AF411568

How to Administrate the Church

Witness Lee

Living Stream Ministry
Anaheim, CA • www.lsm.org

First Edition, March 2005.

ISBN 0-7363-2838-6

Published by

Living Stream Ministry
2431 W. La Palma Ave., Anaheim, CA 92801 U.S.A.
P. O. Box 2121, Anaheim, CA 92814 U.S.A.

Printed in the United States of America

05 06 07 08 09 10 11 / 9 8 7 6 5 4 3 2 1

CONTENTS

PREFACE

This book is a collection of messages given by Witness Lee in 1952 related to the service of the church. It contains nine messages concerning what the church is, the building and administration of the church, the materials of God's work, and the proper prayer and faith of a serving one. These messages are translated from the original Chinese.

CHAPTER ONE

WHAT THE CHURCH IS

(1)

Scripture Reading: 1 Tim. 3:15-16; Eph. 1:19-23

First Timothy 3:15-16 says, "But if I delay, I write that you may know how one ought to conduct himself in the house of God, which is the church of the living God, the pillar and base of the truth. And confessedly, great is the mystery of godliness: He who was manifested in the flesh, / Justified in the Spirit, / Seen by angels, / Preached among the nations, / Believed on in the world, / Taken up in glory." These two verses show that the pillar and base of the truth is the mystery of godliness, which is God manifested in the flesh. In other words, the house spoken of here is the church of the living God, the pillar and base of the truth, and the mystery of godliness, which is God manifested in the flesh. Then the apostle continues by saying that God, who was manifested in the flesh, was "justified in the Spirit, / Seen by angels, / Preached among the nations, / Believed on in the world, / Taken up in glory." All of these items refer to the Lord Jesus Himself.

Ephesians 1:19-20 says, "What is the surpassing greatness of His power toward us who believe, according to the operation of the might of His strength, which He caused to operate in Christ in raising Him from the dead and seating Him at His right hand in the heavenlies." The power spoken of here is of two sides, one on the negative side, and the other on the positive side. On the negative side, this power raised the Lord from the dead, and on the positive side, this power seated the Lord at the right hand of God in the heavenlies.

Verse 21 says, "Far above all rule and authority and power and lordship and every name that is named not only in this age but also in that which is to come." It seems that the Lord's ascension is a matter of space—from earth to heaven, but verse 21 shows that the Lord's ascension is also a matter of time. He not only ascended far above the earth with respect to space, but He also transcended this age, the past ages, and the age to come with respect to time. His transcending over space and time is the result of His ascension.

Verse 22 continues, "And He subjected all things under His feet and gave Him to be Head over all things to the church." *Far above* in verse 21 refers to Christ's being far above Satan and his angels. *Rule, authority, power, lordship,* and *every name that is named not only in this age but also in that which is to come* refer to the power of darkness. Christ transcends all of them. Moreover, God has subjected all things under Christ's feet; *all things* refers to all created things. Giving Him to be Head over all things is the issue of Christ's transcendency.

Verse 23 says, "Which [the church] is His Body, the fullness of the One who fills all in all." Here it clearly says that the church is the Body of Christ, the fullness of the One who fills all in all.

KNOWING WHAT THE CHURCH IS

The responsible brothers in many local churches are very concerned about the matter of how to administrate the church. However, in order to administrate the church, we must first know what the church is. This is a simple truth. No matter what thing a person studies, he must first know its nature, use, and purpose. In order to administrate an organization or a company, we must first know its nature, use, and purpose. Whether it is a family, a shopping mall, a factory, a school, an orphanage, a home for the elderly, or even a jail, if we want to administrate an organization, we must first know its nature, use, and purpose. In the same way, in order to administrate the church, we must know what the church is, including the nature and function of the church and the purpose of the establishment of the church in the universe. We must have a fundamental understanding, because only then can we know what it means to administrate the church and how to administrate it.

We often see someone administrating the church in a faithful way, and we may not even sense an improper spirit in him. It is sad, however, if he does not truly know the church even though he is administrating the church. He is like a founder of a school who does not know that the purpose of a school is for education. He administrates the church, but he does not know the church, the nature of the church, or the origin of the church. This is a very solemn matter. If we want to know how to administrate the church, we must spend much time in the Lord's Word to see, according to the Lord's revelation, what the church is, what the purpose of the church is, and what the function of the church is in the universe.

KNOWING HOW TO CONDUCT ONESELF
IN THE HOUSE OF GOD

We must consider the administration of the church with the Scriptures as our basis. First Timothy 3:15 says, "If I delay, I write that you may know how one ought to conduct himself in the house of God, which is the church of the living God." Here *conduct* refers to administration. Paul wrote to Timothy, and Timothy received Paul's commission to arrange for matters related to the management and administration of the churches. When Paul spoke of knowing "how one ought to conduct himself in the house of God," he was speaking of how to administrate and arrange matters in the church. Paul said this because he knew that he might be absent for a long period of time, that he might be delayed. Therefore, he wanted Timothy to know how to administrate the church and how to conduct himself in the church. It may seem that Paul was speaking only about being delayed himself, but if we have spiritual insight, we will realize that he was actually referring to the Lord being delayed. Before the Lord comes back, we must know how to administrate the church and how to conduct ourselves in the church. This is the only verse in the entire Bible which clearly speaks of administrating the church and conducting ourselves in the church.

THE CHURCH BEING THE HOUSE OF GOD

Concerning the matter of administrating and taking care of the church, we first must see what the church is. The church is the house of God. The church is not an organization, a company, a school, a factory, or a hospital; rather, the church is a house—the house of God. We must know this house in a strong and deep way. All matters and their proper order in the universe, such as parents and children in a family and employers and employees in a company, are arranged by God and are of God. All such arrangements have symbolic meaning. The father in a family signifies God as the Father, the children signify the saved ones as the children of God, and the family as a whole signifies the house of God. If we want to know the significance of the church as the house of God, we can understand it by looking at our own family, because God has presented this significance before our eyes through His arrangement of human relationships. Under normal circumstances, everyone should have his own home; a proper home is a symbol of the house of God.

The House of God Being a Place for the Continuation of God's Life

Concerning the function of a family, everyone in a proper family, whether children or parents, all have some understanding. A proper family should at least cause man to have inward and outward rest. Moreover, a family is a place for the multiplication and the continuation of life. There are hardly any couples who feel that they do not need children. Everyone hopes to have many children and grandchildren when they reach an advanced age. The older a person is, the more he longs to see that his children have grown up and the more he likes to speak about his children and grandchildren.

Similarly, God delights in the continuation of His life. The reason that God has a family is because He wants to have children. Although some families do not have children for biological reasons, in fact and in principle, a family is called a family because it is a place where children are produced. Whether we agree or not, this is what God has ordained.

Children are the multiplication and continuation of life. Hence, to God the first significance of a family is to enable God's life to be multiplied and continued. This is the symbolic meaning of a family, showing that God's house is a place for the continuation and multiplication of life. This is the only place in the universe where life can be multiplied and continued. This is the first significance of a house.

When we touch God's house, we touch the matter of God's life, because a family is where life is continued. Chinese people like to have children because they want to transmit life and produce offspring. God needs a household for the continuation of His life. This life is not a hidden life but a generating life. Before we are married, our life is hidden, but once we are married, we begin to generate life. Sixteen years ago when I was in Tientsin, a brother came to my house. Upon seeing my children, he said, "Each one of them is a 'small Witness Lee.'" Before I was married, there was only one Witness Lee; however, after I was married, there are many Witness Lees. Similarly, one day God will be able to boast in front of His enemy in the universe, saying, "Formerly, there was only Myself, but now I have become so many." God's house is where His life is continued.

Some people may say, "This is the definition of a house according to symbolic meaning, but is there a scriptural basis for this?" Yes! First Timothy 3:15 says, "Which [the house] is the church of the living God." God is a living God. *Living* denotes a matter of life. Is there a living tree that does not bear fruit? Is there a living animal that does not produce offspring? As long as something is living, whether it is an animal or a plant, it surely will produce offspring and bear fruit. Anything that lives is capable of generating life. We can have children and propagate life because we are living. Our God is not the God of the dead but the God of the living; hence, in His house He wants to propagate His life.

The House of God Being a Place
for the Expression of God Himself

Second, a house is for expression and manifestation. No other place expresses ourself more than our own home. We can see the true condition of a person in his home. What we cannot tell others and what we are embarrassed to say before others can be said at home. What we cannot make public in other places can be made public at home. Hence, our home is the best place for us to express ourselves. The place where we feel the most comfortable and free is in our home. The church is the house of God, where God's life is propagated and where God Himself is expressed. God's desires and inclinations are expressed in His house.

If God did not have a home in the universe, He would not have a place to propagate His life; if God did not have a home in the universe, He would not have a place to express and manifest Himself, thereby showing forth His mystery. There is no place like the church in which God can speak and show forth Himself. If the church is not this way, it shows that she has lost sight of her nature. If we must keep quiet and are not allowed to speak a word in our home, then our home is just like a court of law. The church is where God can pour Himself out.

The House of God Being a Place for God to Rest

Third, a house is a resting place; there is affection and love in a home. There is care, sympathy, and the sweetness of human relationships in a home. The sweetness of human relationships can be tasted only in a home. If a home has been corrupted by Satan, the enjoyment of human relationships is annulled. Hence, the most serious thing that Satan does in human relationships is to corrupt the family. All the enjoyment and meaning of human relationships are in the home. A home is a place for one to express his emotions and to rest. Only when a person has a home can he find rest inwardly and outwardly. It is the same with the church. If God did not have the church in the universe, He would have no rest. Without the church, God does not have a place that can respond to His love and His heart. This house is where God rests.

The church as the house of God is for the continuation of God's life, the expression and manifestation of God, and the rest of God. If we know the church in this way, we will know how to conduct ourselves in the church. The way we act in the church must enable God to propagate His life, to express Himself, and to have rest. This is our action based upon our knowledge of the church.

I spoke about this matter in Canton four years ago, because at that time I saw a situation in which the brothers and sisters had many opinions whenever they came together to serve. I sensed that it was not like the house of God but more like a legislature. When the brothers and sisters sat there, they were all like legislators, and they did not give any room for God to express Himself. Therefore, when they asked me questions about the church, I said that the church is the house of God and that we must allow God to speak. If the master of a house does not have the ground to speak in his own home, the home must not be proper.

In all of the ways that we conduct ourselves, we must firmly grasp the principle that the church is the house of God. Our conduct in the church must be restricted by these principles. We should not do anything that hinders God's life from being propagated, and we need to stop things that prevent God from speaking and being expressed; otherwise, the nature of God's house will be ruined. Moreover, we must let God have rest in the church.

THE CHURCH BEING
THE PILLAR AND BASE OF THE TRUTH

According to 1 Timothy 3:15, the house of God is the church of the living God, the pillar and base of the truth. The church is the house of the living God; the church is also the pillar and base of the truth. First, we need to see what *truth* refers to in this verse, because this is a great matter. The truth spoken of in this verse is "He who was manifested in the flesh" in the following verse. John 1:1 says, "In the beginning was the Word, and the Word was with God, and the Word was God." Then verse 14 continues, "And the Word became flesh and tabernacled among us..., full of grace and reality [truth]." We know that this truth has become flesh, because verse 17 says, "Grace and reality [truth] came through Jesus Christ." John 14:6 says, "I am...the reality [truth]." This One is the God who created all things and who became flesh. Hence, *truth* refers to God entering into man.

Truth is God being manifested in man; the joining of God and man is truth. Someone may ask, "Why is the joining of God and man truth?" We should not say that God is truth; rather, God becoming flesh and entering into man is truth, because without God being added, all the created things are false and empty. For example, an electric lamp without electricity is a false and hollow lamp. Only when electricity enters into the electric lamp can it be real and true. God is the reality of all things, just as electricity is the reality of the electric lamp. Electricity itself does not need to become real, because it is real. Likewise, our spirit and soul are the reality of our body as a shell; if our spirit and soul leave, our body becomes a sham. God must enter into human beings so that they may have the reality in them. Hence, truth refers to God's entering into man, that is, the Creator's entering into His creatures. This is called truth, which is the manifestation of God in the flesh.

The truth of God being manifested in the flesh is upheld by the church. The church is the pillar and the base of this truth. The church is too great; God manifested in the flesh is a great matter. The Bible says, "Great is the mystery of godliness" (1 Tim. 3:16). This great matter is upheld by the church. The church is the pillar and base of God being manifested in the flesh, and this matter needs to be upheld by the church. When we see the church, we see the manifestation of God in the flesh. If the church is not present, the manifestation of God is finished.

This reminds us of what the Lord Jesus said in Matthew 16:18: "Upon this rock I will build My church." We all know that Christ is the rock, the foundation, upon which the church is built. When we come to 1 Timothy, however, we see that the church becomes the base of God's manifestation in the flesh. The fact of this mystery rests with the church. The church is the pillar and base of this matter. A pillar denotes support, which can be seen in the beams of a house which are supported by pillars. However, with regard to the truth of God being manifested in the flesh, the church is not only the pillar but also the base. This shows that the church upholds and presents the matter of God's manifestation in the flesh to the universe in time and space. God entrusts this mystery to the church. If we see this, we will confess that the administration of the church is a great matter.

All who serve God in the church, all who work for the Lord, all who preach the gospel, and all who administrate the church must be brought by the Lord to such a high realm to see that the church is the pillar and base of the truth, upholding the fact of God's manifestation in the universe. This is a great and mysterious matter. Without this vision, we will not know what we are doing. A day must come when our eyes are opened to see that the church we serve and administrate is such a great matter; only then will we know what we are doing. What we do is too great and too mysterious!

THE MYSTERY OF GODLINESS

First Timothy 3:16 says, "Great is the mystery of godliness." The mystery of godliness is the mystery of God entering into man and being joined to man. At the same time, this mystery is godly. The definition of *godly* in a Bible lexicon is "godlikeness, being like God." *Godliness* is a biblical term, which is related to our word *godlikeness* or *being like God*. The more we have God's likeness in our living, the more we are like God; the more we live like God, the more godly we are. A godly person is one who is like God. Hence, whenever we read about godliness in the Bible, we should think of godlikeness. The mystery of God being manifested is the mystery of man being like God. The mystery of God entering into His creatures is the mystery of godliness. When we do not have this mystery, we are not like God. But if we have the mystery of God being manifested in the flesh and of men of flesh being joined to God, then we, as men of flesh, can be like God. This is godliness, and this is also a mystery.

If we tell people that we have God in us, they may say that we are crazy, because this matter is truly too great a mystery. The world does not know, see, or understand this matter. God becoming flesh is a great mystery. When the Lord Jesus was on the earth, He was a mystery. Outwardly speaking, He was a Jew who grew up in Nazareth, but inwardly there was a story that was not yet manifested—there was still a mystery. One day He died and entered into death; then the mystery was manifested. After He was resurrected and ascended, He, as the Holy Spirit, entered into us, and thus we also became part of the mystery.

When we preach the gospel, we testify to people that we have a treasure in us which even the noblest man in the world cannot obtain (2 Cor. 4:7). When Jesus the Nazarene was on earth, He was a mystery among men. Today Christians are also a mystery among men, a mystery incomprehensible to men. When they see us breaking bread, singing, praising, and praying together, they say, "These people are crazy; they sing and shout, and they give thanks and offer praises. What have they really seen?" They neither know nor understand what we are doing. This is the mystery of God manifested in the flesh.

THE CHURCH BEING
GOD MANIFESTED IN THE FLESH

We all know that the church is God manifested in the flesh. The life we propagate represents ourselves. When people see our children, they more or less can tell whose children they are, because our children somewhat look like us. The Fukienese like to have children. It is not enough for them to beget one, but they also are willing to adopt another one. But there is a difference between a begotten child and an adopted child. For example, Brother Lin has a biological child whose surname is Lin, and he has adopted two children, who also have the surname Lin. If all three children were here, we could distinguish between his biological child and his adopted children simply by looking at them. A child is an expression of the one who has begotten him. The church is the house of God, the place where God is, so it is the manifestation of God in the flesh. In this house we can see God, not an individual God but God who is in His children, that is, in many men of the flesh. This is the church.

Whenever we meet, we are the manifestation of God in the flesh. When people see that our meetings are so good, they say that God indeed is among us (1 Cor. 14:25). God is among us; we truly have God in our meetings. Every saved one is God's manifestation in the flesh. When some people see that we meet every day, they wonder how we can take it. But they do not realize that we cannot live without meeting. Once we get off from work, we go to the meeting hall. This is something mysterious and surprising in man's eyes. The church is not a meeting hall; the church is God manifested in the flesh, the house of God, the place where God's life is propagated. This is a great mystery, a mystery of godliness.

Moreover, 1 Timothy 3:16 says, "Justified in the Spirit, / Seen by angels, / Preached among the nations, / Believed on in the world, / Taken up in glory." These five matters speak of Christ and also the church. Christ is the individual manifestation of God in the flesh, and the church is the corporate manifestation of God in the flesh. The Head of the manifestation of God in the flesh is Christ, and the Body of this manifestation is the church; only when the two—the Head and the Body—are joined together can the manifestation be complete. Hence, this verse refers both to Christ and the church. God being manifested in the flesh means that Christ is in this manifestation. These five matters do not refer only to Christ or only to the church. Instead, they speak of Christ and the church together because the two cannot be separated. Hence, when we preach Christ, we preach the church because the church is Christ.

Some people say that we have lost our vigor for gospel preaching and that we like to listen only to messages about Christ and the cross and want only to see revelation. This raises a question about the power of our gospel preaching. If the fervor and excitement of our gospel preaching in the past was of Christ, then the release of messages on Christ and the cross should make us even more fervent to preach the gospel. But if the power of our gospel preaching was a replacement of Christ, then when Christ is manifested among us, the replacement will fade away. The proper gospel preaching is for the church, as Christ, to preach Christ. When we are telling people to believe in Christ, the church in reality is also telling people to believe in the church. Verse 16 says, "He who was… / Preached among the nations, / Believed on in the world." The church, however, is not preached among the nations, nor is the church believed on in the world; rather, *Christ* is preached among the nations and believed on in the world.

There are two ways to preach Christ: one is to preach the Christ who died, resurrected, and ascended, and the other is to preach the Christ who died, resurrected, ascended, and is now living in us. One way is to preach the ascended Christ, and the other is to preach the Christ who lives in us. "For to me, to live is Christ" (Phil. 1:21). Because Christ lives in us (Gal. 2:20), we are Christ. When we preach the gospel, we are Christ, and all that we preach is Christ. If this is the case, our gospel preaching will have another flavor, and the more we listen to messages on Christ and the cross, the more we will preach the gospel.

ONE WHO PREACHES CHRIST BEING CHRIST

In Acts, those who preached the gospel, who preached Christ, were Christ; even the churches that preached Christ were Christ. Only when we see this can we understand the book of Acts. In Acts the twelve apostles, the one hundred twenty, and Stephen were preaching Christ, but they were also Christ. Can the one hundred twenty be separated from Christ? Can we separate Stephen from Christ? This is why Saul heard a voice out of heaven, saying, "Why are you persecuting Me?" when he met Christ (Acts 9:4). When Saul was persecuting Stephen and other Christians, he was persecuting "Me"; when Saul was persecuting the church, he was persecuting "Me."

Those who preached Christ were Christ; the churches and the apostles who preached Christ were Christ. We need to see that those who preached the gospel in Acts, who preached Christ, were Christ. When Christ was believed on in the world, they were believed on in the world; when Christ was preached among the nations, they were preached among the nations; when Christ was seen by angels, they were seen by angels; when Christ was taken up in glory, they were taken up in glory. Christ was joined to them, and Christ lived in them; therefore, to them, to live was Christ. We must be very clear in this matter; otherwise, we will not know what we are doing in the church.

We need to pray that God would show us what the church is in nature, function, and content. The church is the house of the living God, it is where His life is propagated, where He can express and manifest Himself, and where He finds rest. Moreover, the church is God manifested in the flesh. Great is the mystery of godliness because the church is one with Christ and mingled with Christ; it was this way in the past, and it is still this way in the present. The church is justified in the Spirit, seen by angels, preached among the nations, believed on in the world, and taken up in glory. This is the church.

In order for us to administrate the church, we must see the church. This is what the Holy Spirit is conveying in 1 Timothy 3:15-16. If we want to administrate and serve the church, we must see that the church is such a great matter. We must see this so that we will know how we ought to conduct ourselves in the church if the Lord delays His coming.

WHAT THE CHURCH IS

(2)

Scripture Reading: Eph. 1:19-23

There are two portions in the New Testament that speak of the church; one is at the end of 1 Timothy 3, and the other is at the end of Ephesians 1. In addition to these two portions, it is difficult to find another that speaks of the church in such a high and deep way. Hence, if we want to know the church, we must come to these two portions. In the preceding chapter we have seen the church from the viewpoint of 1 Timothy 3; now we need to see the church from the viewpoint of Ephesians 1.

In 1:19-22, Paul says, "What is the surpassing greatness of His power toward us who believe, according to the operation of the might of His strength, which He caused to operate in Christ in raising Him from the dead and seating Him at His right hand in the heavenlies, far above all rule and authority and power and lordship and every name that is named not only in this age but also in that which is to come; and He subjected all things under His feet and gave Him to be Head over all things to the church." This shows how the church is produced and how the church exists in the universe. As a concluding word, verse 23 says, "Which is His Body, the fullness of the One who fills all in all." This shows what the church is. The church is the Body of Christ, the fullness of the One who fills all in all.

The church is produced by Christ's being raised from the dead, ascending to heaven, transcending the limitations of time and space, overcoming all the enemies, and having all things subjected under His feet. The church is produced through these steps. Thus, we must clearly see that without Christ's resurrection, there would be no church; without Christ's ascension, there would be no church; without Christ's transcending of time and space, there would be no church; without Christ's overcoming all rule and authority, there would be no church. In Ephesians 6:12, *rulers* and *authorities* refer to Satan and his angels. Therefore, the rulers and the authorities spoken of in Ephesians and Colossians do not refer to kings and high officials of the world but to Satan and his authorities (Eph. 1:21; 6:12; Col. 1:13, 16). To be far above all rule and authority means to be far above the power of darkness of Satan. Without this transcendence, the church would not exist. Without Christ's having all things subjected under His feet, the church would not exist. Without Christ's being given to be Head over all things, the church would not exist. We must see the six characteristics of the church in order to clearly see how the church is produced.

THE CHURCH BEING PRODUCED
THROUGH CHRIST'S RESURRECTION

The church is produced through Christ's resurrection (Eph. 1:20). Christ came out of death through the power of resurrection; the issue of His resurrection is the producing of the church. Resurrection is the release of the infinite life of God from the shell of the created humanity which Christ entered. When He was incarnated, He entered into a created shell, and the unlimited life in Him was restricted in this created shell. Hence, in Luke 12:50 the Lord said, "But I have a baptism to be baptized with, and how I am pressed until it is accomplished!" Before He passed through death, He was pressed. When He entered into the created shell, the infinite life in Him was restricted.

The Lord Jesus entered into death so that through death, the unlimited and infinite life in Him could come out from His created shell. This is the meaning of being raised from the dead. Coming out of death enables life to be released (John 12:24). Formerly, this life was in God. Then through incarnation this life entered into a created person. This created One was Jesus the Nazarene; He became a grain of wheat. He died and resurrected so that the infinite life might come out of His finite shell. Through death and resurrection, His life entered into many created ones, including Peter, James, John, and even you and me. Hence, His resurrection produced the church.

The producing of the church is based on Christ's death and resurrection. The church is an entity that has passed through death and resurrection. The central significance of death and resurrection is that the life of God, which entered into one of His creatures, has been released and has entered into even more of His creatures. Moreover, there is another meaning to death and resurrection. Death delivers man from everything of the old creation, and resurrection ushers man into God's new creation, into God's life (2 Cor. 5:17; Gal. 6:15). All of the old creation, which is natural, defiled, and fallen, has been thoroughly dealt with by Christ's death. This is the reason we can say that Christ's death delivers man from everything of the old creation, and Christ's resurrection brings man into the glorious life of God. It is this glorious life that produces the new creation.

This shows that anything that has not passed through death is of the old creation and is natural. However, what is of resurrection is God's life, is in God's life, and has entered into the glorious life of God (Luke 24:26; John 1:13; 3:15). The church is produced through Christ's death and resurrection. Thus, the church is not in the natural life or in the old creation, but in God's life and in the new creation.

THE CHURCH BEING PRODUCED
THROUGH CHRIST'S ASCENSION

The church is produced through Christ's ascension (Eph. 1:20). To ascend is to leave the earth completely. Whereas the earth is where Satan moves and rules, heaven is where God rules. In Matthew 6:10 the Lord Jesus taught His disciples to pray: "Your will be done, as in heaven, so also on earth." This shows that God's will is done more easily in heaven than on earth. Heaven is where God rules and where His will is done; however, it is more difficult for God to rule and for His will to be done on earth, because the earth has fallen into Satan's usurpation. In the Bible, from Genesis 3 onward, any reference to the earth implies that the earth is under the authority of Satan and belongs to him.

In the Bible the serpent signifies Satan (Rev. 12:9), because the serpent creeps on the earth and is joined to the earth. Leviticus says that swarming locusts and swallowing locusts are clean, because they can fly and go above the earth (11:21-22). All the swarming things that swarm on the earth, however, are unclean (v. 29). This difference in the physical sense also has spiritual significance. After man fell through Satan's temptation, from God's perspective the earth was altogether trampled by Satan and possessed by him. Therefore, God cursed the serpent so that it would not walk with legs but would go upon its stomach and eat dust all the days of its life (Gen. 3:14). In His ascension the Lord left the earth; He left everything that belonged to the earth. Every time the earth is spoken of after Genesis chapter 3, we need to realize that Satan is implied. Heaven belongs to God, and the earth belongs to Satan. The church was not produced when the Lord was on the earth; rather, the church was produced in the realm of heaven after the Lord's ascension, after He had absolutely departed from the earth. Although the church is on earth, her nature is not earthly but heavenly, because she was produced by the One who is in heaven. Hence, the church is not earthly but heavenly.

THE CHURCH SURPASSING THE POWER OF DARKNESS

Through the Lord's ascension, He surpassed the power of the darkness of the rulers and authorities on earth and in the air (Eph. 1:21). After the earth was trampled and usurped by Satan, Ephesians 2:2 indicates that the air also belongs to Satan. Through ascension, the Lord Jesus surpassed Satan who is on the earth and in the air. Once He surpassed these things, He produced the church. The One who produced the church is far above Satan, who is on the earth and in the air. We may not have ever considered that the church is far above Satan. On the contrary, we often sink into our own feeling, especially when the church is under persecution, thinking that the church will not overcome the authority of Satan but instead will be subject to it. When the church is weak and is under attack, we often feel that Satan has defeated the church. This shows that we have not seen clearly that the church is far above the authority of Satan.

The church is produced by the ascended One in heaven. This ascended One is far above Satan and the position and boundary of his rule. Ephesians 1:21 does not say that the Lord Jesus is far above Satan but that He is "far above all rule and authority and power and lordship and every name that is named not only in this age but also in that which is to come." This implies that not only is the Lord far above Satan, time, and space but that the church is produced in the Lord's transcendence. The church is also far above Satan and far above the time and space that belong to Satan. The church is produced far above Satan and even far above his time and space.

THE CHURCH TRANSCENDING TIME AND SPACE

Christ's ascension causes the church not only to transcend the limitations of time and space but also to transcend time and space itself. The church is produced outside of time and space (v. 21). Hence, the church is exceedingly great and exceedingly high. In the past our knowledge of the church was too low, and our knowledge of Christ was too inadequate. We did not know that the church was so great and high. I hope from now on we will realize that the church transcends time and space. The church is neither in time nor in space; rather, she is produced outside of time and space.

THE CHURCH BEING FAR ABOVE ALL THINGS

The church is far above all things. When Christ ascended to the heavenlies, not only was He far above Satan, time, and space, but also all things were subjected under His feet (v. 22). The church was produced because Christ is not only above all things but also because all things have been put under His feet. Hence, the church is above all things, and all things are under the feet of the church. The church is produced from the One who is the Head over all things because all things are under His feet.

THE CHURCH BEING THE HEAD OVER ALL THINGS IN ITS UNION WITH CHRIST

The church is also the head over all things because it is joined to Christ. Ephesians 1:22 says, "And gave Him to be Head over all things to the church." When Christ produced the church, He was the Head over all things. In other words, the church was produced out of Christ's being the Head over all things; hence, the church, along with Christ, is also the head over all things.

The church is not in the old creation but in the new creation of God's life; the church is not of the earth but of heaven; the church surpasses Satan; the church transcends time and space; the church is far above all things; and the church, being above all, follows Christ her Head to be the head over all things and to rule over all things. It is only at this point in Ephesians that Paul draws a final conclusion regarding the church. His conclusion consists of two points: the church is "the Body of Christ" and "the fullness of the One who fills all in all" (v. 23). At this stage, the church is Christ; the church is the extension and enlargement of Christ, just as the body is the extension and the fullness of the head. The church is not only joined to Christ, but it is also the overflow of Christ.

All the saved ones in the church were once part of the "all things," but when we were saved, we became far above all things and were joined to the Head over all things to experience Him as the Head over all things to the church. We need to firmly grasp these six characteristics of the church in order to understand the conclusion of Ephesians 1: the church is not of the old creation, not earthly, not under the authority of Satan, not in time or space, and not among all things but above all things as the head over all things with Christ. When we see these items, we will have some understanding of the church.

FOUR ITEMS OF WHAT THE CHURCH IS AND SIX CHARACTERISTICS OF THE CHURCH

First Timothy 3 shows that the church is the house of God. A house is where one's life is propagated, where one can express himself, and where one can find rest. The church is also the pillar and base of the truth. The truth is God being manifested in the flesh. The manifestation of God in the flesh is the "great mystery of godliness," which causes the church to be mingled with Christ as one. Therefore, when we preach the church, we preach Christ. First Timothy 3:16 speaks of five matters: justified in the Spirit, seen by angels, preached among the nations, believed on in the world, and taken up in glory. These five matters show that the church is mingled with Christ and cannot be separated from Christ. The church is Christ, and Christ is the church; the two have become one. Then according to Ephesians 1, we see that the church is the Body of Christ and the fullness of the One who fills all in all.

The church, as the fullness of the One who fills all in all, has six characteristics. First, the church is not the old creation but the new creation of God's life. Second, the church is not earthly but heavenly. Third, the church is not under the authority of Satan but is far above Satan. Fourth, the church is not in time and space but transcends time and space. Fifth, the church is not part of the "all things" but is above all things. Sixth, the church is not under all things but above all things and experiences being the head over all things with Christ. We can administrate the church only after we have seen these items clearly. Our actions, our management, our viewpoint, our discernment, our decisions, and our proposals all must be according to the four items of what the church is: the house of God, the pillar and base of the truth, the Body of Christ, and the fullness of the One who fills all in all.

OUR VISION OF THE CHURCH
GOVERNING THE WAY WE CONDUCT OURSELVES
IN THE CHURCH

As we are serving and administrating in a certain local church, do we have a strong feeling that we should not bring anything into the church that is of the old creation, that is of the earth, that is not far above Satan, and that is in time and space? Do we have a solemn feeling that because the church is heavenly and above all things, transcending time and space, that we should not bring anything of the earth and of the old creation into the church? We need to fear God, please

God, and do what is according to His will. In the church everything must be according to His will, and we must reject anything that is not according to His will. When we handle a matter in the church, we should pray, "O God, what should we do to be according to Your will? We want what is according to Your will, and we reject what is not according to Your will." What is according to God's will can be determined by the four items of what the church is and the six characteristics of the church.

Perhaps we do not have a deep and weighty feeling regarding the four items of what the church is and the six characteristics of the church; instead, we may only feel that we must please God and obey His will in a general way. However, Ephesians 1 clearly shows the significance of the church. Hence, in all of our actions in the church, such as making decisions, handling affairs, and taking care of various matters, we must not bring in anything that is of the old creation, that is earthly, that is of time and space, that is of Satan, and that is of the flesh. This may be likened to the work of a jeweler who cannot mix any other elements with gold because he knows that he is making gold jewelry. Unless he wants to deceive people, he cannot mix in any impurities, such as bronze or silver, into the gold. Our administration of the church will be pure, and our discernment, decisions, proposals, and conduct will be purified only when we see the light concerning the church in 1 Timothy 3 and Ephesians 1.

If we have truly seen that the church is the house of God, the place where God expresses Himself, we dare not and will not speak casually when we speak concerning how to manage the affairs of the church. However, if we do not see this vision, I will express my views, you will express your feelings, and another will express his opinions whenever we discuss the affairs of the church. What is this? This is clearly not the house of God. If we have seen that the church is the house of God and that we are stewards in this house, we will not voice our opinions or speak as we please. For example, we may have a servant who knows how to do things and how to manage the affairs of the house very well. However, if he also has many ideas and opinions, we will not like to use him because our house would become his house.

If we have seen that the church is the house of God, the place where God expresses Himself, then when we touch the matters of the church, we will stop our speaking and our opinions. Everything we do must be according to this principle. The church is the house of the living God for the propagation of God's life. When we handle church affairs, we must take this into consideration and take this as a principle. Sometimes the saints see the church only as a school for education rather than for the propagation of God's life. All of our actions, decisions, and administration in the church must be governed by our knowledge of the church. Thus, I deeply sense before the Lord that we must first know what the church is in order for us to know how to administrate the church. When we see what the church is, our actions in the church will be governed by what we have seen. If we want to know how to conduct ourselves in the church, we must see what the church is. All of our views, methods, talents, and learning avail nothing. Our administration, our conduct, in the church must be according to our knowledge of the church.

The church is not in the old creation but in the new creation. Hence, we cannot decide things in the church according to the old creation, and we cannot observe things in the church according to the view of the old creation. The church is heavenly; therefore, we cannot decide things in the church according to an earthly view. If we decide things in the church according to an earthly view, we do not consider the church to be heavenly. I am afraid that even though many saints are clear about this truth, they may not know how to apply it.

For example, recently the church in Manila decided to buy a big piece of land, which cost about US$150,000. When construction costs were included, it was close to 250,000 dollars. However, so far they have received less than 12,500 dollars from offerings, even though the transaction of the land has been closed for a few months. Since the offerings received by the church were not sufficient, funds from other sources have been temporarily advanced to the church. Hence, the elders feel that this is a burden.

When the church in Manila first began to build a meeting hall, the typical practice was to gather a few wealthy saints, form them into a committee for the construction of the hall, and then lay the burden on them. If there was a need for 30,000 dollars, the committee members would decide that one would give 5,000, another would give 10,000, and a third would give 15,000. Then they would write and sign checks for the needed amount. When they needed to pay another 30,000 dollars, they still signed checks in the end, even though the committee brothers had prayed, "O Lord, You accomplish this for us." One would give 10,000, another 5,000, and still another gave 15,000 to cover the required payment.

After they bought the new piece of land, the elders asked me what they should do. I told them that they did not need a committee or committee members as long as someone could handle matters in the church. I also said, "You must be clear that when you gather the brothers and sisters to pray, your prayers must be for God's ears. If you pray with the intention of exhorting the brothers and sisters to give, this will not be acceptable." I told them that they should not organize a construction committee or use prayers for exhortation. Hence, they received offerings of only about 12,500 dollars.

This matter stayed this way for several months, and I did not say a thing because this was not my business but the Lord's. But because the responsible brothers could not take it for very long, they held a meeting in secret and said, "If Brother Lee will come and fellowship with a few brothers, this problem will be resolved." When I visited the church, they did not dare speak to me in the elders' meeting; instead, they spoke to an elderly sister who was giving me hospitality of their desire for me to speak. This sister told me later that she said, "This will not work. You want Brother Lee to speak, but if he will not say a word related to the needs in Taiwan, even though the need there is very great, how do you expect to force him to say something about the need here?" She told me the whole story.

When I was about to leave Manila, I indicated to the elders that if I wanted to organize a Chinese business association or a youth club, I could have raised the funds a long time ago.

However, I could not do this in the church where I serve God and lead the children of God, because this method is earthly. Establishing a construction committee, gathering those among us who are wealthy, and splitting up the costs is the practice of the world; we cannot do this in the church. We must see before the Lord what the church is, and then, when we take any action in the church, we will be standing on the proper ground.

What I have spoken of here is in principle. The church is the house of God, the pillar and base of the truth, the Body of Christ, and the fullness of the One who fills all in all. The church is a new creation; it is not of the old creation. The church surpasses Satan; it is not under his authority. The church transcends time and space; it is not in time and space. The church is above all and is head over all things with Christ. Seeing these items will govern the way we conduct ourselves in the church. We can do many legal and proper things in the world, but we cannot do them in the church because the church is different in her nature. We must have this vision of the church; then we will conduct ourselves properly in the church.

QUESTIONS AND ANSWERS

Question: How does the church transcend time and space, and how is it far above all things?

Answer: Let us use an illustration. In the church life in Taipei, hall one always wants hall one to do well, hall two wants hall two to do well, and hall three wants hall three to do well. Every meeting hall wants its own hall to be the best. When we speak of the arrangement for the service and material furnishings, every meeting hall competes with the others. For example, if we want to transfer the service of some brothers to Keelung, the brothers in the church in Keelung immediately say, "We really need them." However, brothers from other churches say that they also are short of hands. So they begin to quarrel. The only reason that they quarrel is because they have not seen that the church transcends space. There is no such thing as the church that belongs to Keelung, to Kaohsiung, to Taipei hall one, or to Taipei hall two. Although there are local churches on the earth today, they are temporary. The church transcends time and space. Our eyes need to be opened to see that when the church in Keelung is not doing well, the church in Kaohsiung also is not doing well; when the church in Keelung is strong, the church in Kaohsiung also is strong; when hall one in Taipei is rich spiritually, hall two also is rich spiritually. The church transcends time and space.

Several days ago, when we were reading a publication put out by a certain group, we noticed that they used almost all of the spiritual terms that we use. From the time Christianity came to China, no one ever used the term *prayer and fellowship meeting;* we were the first. However, the schedule of meetings printed in this publication included a "prayer and fellowship meeting." Moreover, there was also an article that spoke about coordination in the service, that is, the brothers and sisters being coordinated in the service of the Body.

When we come to the Lord and consider this matter, we should sense inwardly that we have been blessed to see something and have invented some spiritual terms. Now other people, because of their seeing, are also using our terms. Because the children of God have been blessed, we should be inwardly peaceful. For instance, some people borrow our gospel training materials and produce Christians who know how to preach the gospel; we should praise the Lord. Even though they do not take this way, God is also blessing them with our messages. We should bow our heads and worship Him. If we see that the church transcends time and space, we will say, "O Lord, I praise You that this is the church. Although C. H. Spurgeon did not stand on the same ground that we do, he is still our brother; although D. L. Moody did not take the same way that we do, he is still our brother. Hallelujah! We are all the church." In this way, many problems will vanish.

We do not merely sit back, wanting Christianity to remain in confusion; rather, we have been praying to the Lord desperately, "O Lord, vindicate Yourself." Even though we pray this way, we can still say, "This is the church. The Lord rules; we do not rule. The Lord intervenes; we do not intervene." If the Lord sees that it is good and fitting for them to do this, what can slaves, who are nothing but dust, say? We can only bow our heads and worship the Lord, saying, "O Lord, this is the church." This is not our work; this is the church. We are here not to build up any so-called church assembly hall, because we know that the church transcends time and space. The apostles Paul, Peter, and John are in the church; so are Luther, Spurgeon, Moody, Finney, and even those whom we do not esteem highly or who take and use the light we see. This is because the church transcends time and space.

In the new heaven and new earth, will we still see the church in Taipei? In the New Jerusalem, will there still be the church in Kaohsiung? Will there still be the churches of the apostolic age? Will there still be the church of the twentieth century? At that time, all the churches in time and space will be gone, having transcended time and space. If we see this, we will become a broad person, and we will know how to conduct ourselves in the church. If, on the contrary, we have not seen this, we will be small-minded and petty. In the New Jerusalem all these problems will be gone. We will all be able to say, "O Lord, the church transcends time and space. As long as people can be blessed, saved, and know You, as long as You can increase in the church, and as long as the Body of Christ can be built up, we have no problem. Even though we could say something, we will not say anything. We worship You because the church is not in time or space." Only when we see this will there be no sectarianism; only when we see this will there be no quarrels.

How then is the church far above all? Since the church is far above all, a church that has a meeting hall is the church and a church that does not have a meeting hall is also the church. Whether the church is the church has nothing to do with having a meeting hall or even having a successful work. The church is far above all, and all things are subjected under her feet. I spoke a strong word to the brothers in Manila, saying, "Concerning the purchase of the land, some elders have said that we do not have money. Others have said that only 12,500 dollars in offerings have been received, and still others have said that we have received checks only in small amounts, but not any large checks. This shows that we have not seen that the church is far above all. If we have seen the church, we would not say such things." If we speak in this way in the church life, we will immediately bring the church into subjection to gold, to mammon. We must realize that the church is far above all. Even if the church is impoverished, she is still far above all.

Hence, if we want to administrate the church, lead the church, and know how to conduct the affairs of the church, we must see what the church is. Otherwise, we will not know how to handle matters in the church, and we will also make the church worthless. The church transcends time and space and is far above all things. First Corinthians 3:21 says, "All things are yours." In other words, all things belong to the church. The church is above all, and the Head of the church is Head over all things to the church. If we truly see this, we will have the faith that when there is a need, the One who is Head over all things to the church will give all things to the church. Since Christ is Head over all things to the church, how can He not cause all things to work together for good to the church? It is a fact that all things are for the church.

When we know the church, we will know how to administrate the church, lead the church, and conduct the affairs of the church. The things we do must be related to not being disobedient to the heavenly vision that we have seen in regard to the church. Only when the Lord gives us the light will we know how to conduct ourselves in the house of God.

CHAPTER THREE

THE BUILDING AND THE ADMINISTRATION OF THE CHURCH

(1)

THE PERFECTING OF THE SAINTS

Scripture Reading: Eph. 4:11-16

Ephesians 4:11-16 is a crucial portion in the Bible; it is also a portion that is difficult to understand. If we want to know how to administrate the church and serve in the church, we must have a thorough knowledge of this portion. First, we must forsake all of our natural concepts from the past regarding the administration of the church. Whenever we do anything, we all have some natural concepts concerning how to proceed and how things should be done. Thus, when we come to the matter of administrating the church, we also have some natural concepts concerning the appropriate way to carry out and manage church affairs. These concepts may have come from our own thoughts or may have been imparted to us by others. In any case, because these concepts are traditional and natural, we should put them aside. At the same time, we need to enter into God's Word and see how to administrate the church and serve in the church.

THE BUILDING UP OF THE BODY OF CHRIST
IN EPHESIANS 4

Although Ephesians 4:11-16 is not easy to study, it has a very clear structure. In this portion Paul speaks of how Christ produced the church and gave gifts to the church after His resurrection and ascension. These gifts are the apostles, prophets, evangelists, and shepherds and teachers spoken of in verse 11. The Lord gave these ones as gifts to the church. The producing of the church is based upon Christ's resurrection and ascension. In order for the ascended Lord to produce and build up the church on the earth, however, He still needs a group of people who are gifts. We need to read chapter 4 and chapter 1 together. Verses 22 and 23 at the end of chapter 1 indicate that the church is produced through Christ's ascension; then chapter 4 shows that after His ascension, Christ produces, establishes, and builds up the church by giving various gifts to the church.

There is a clear picture of this on the day of Pentecost. After ascending to heaven and sitting on the throne of glory, the Lord, who died and resurrected, produced the church. The Head in heaven did not produce the church directly but rather through the twelve apostles on the earth and the one hundred twenty (Acts 1:15; 2:1-4). In addition to these ones, there were prophets, evangelists, and shepherds and teachers. Christ, the Head, equipped these ones and gave them as gifts to the church; then three thousand and five thousand were saved, and they became the church in Jerusalem (vv. 41, 4:4). This shows that through these gifts—the apostles, prophets, evangelists, and shepherds and teachers—the church was produced by the Head. On one hand, the church was produced by the Head; on the other hand, the church was produced *indirectly* by the Head. The Head produced the church through the gifts.

Christ, the Head, gave these gifts for the perfecting of the saints (Eph. 4:11-12). In the Chinese Union Version, verse 12 is rendered, "For the perfecting of the saints, [for] each one to do the work of his ministry, [for] the building up of the Body of Christ." Based on this translation, some people think that *for each one to do the work of his ministry* refers to the gifts in verse 11 doing the work of their ministry for the perfecting of the saints. They do not think that it refers to the gifts perfecting the saints so that each one of the saints may do the work of ministry. There is a great controversy on this point. Those in the Catholic Church probably think that this verse refers to each of the gifts doing their work to perfect the saints; this is the reason the Catholic Church has a pope, bishops, priests, and monks, each one doing his work to build up the church. According to the rendition of the Chinese Union Version, there might be two interpretations. If *each one to do the work of his ministry* refers to the gifts, the Catholic system is right. In actuality, however, the translation in the Chinese Union Version leans toward the meaning that each of the saints is doing the work of ministry, because verse 16 goes on to say, "Through every joint of the rich supply and through the operation in the measure of each one part, causes the growth of the Body unto the building up of itself in love." In this verse, whereas *every joint of the rich supply* refers to the gifts, *each one part* refers to each of the saints as members of the Body.

According to this portion in the Bible, the Lord's workers should not replace the saints in the church service. In some churches, the workers have been replacing the saints in the service for years. Although these churches have been delivered from the ground of the denominations, they have co-workers among them replacing the saints and doing all the service for them. In the Baptist denomination there are pastors, preachers, elders, and deacons, but generally speaking, almost all the services are under the control of the pastors and preachers. Let us use the board of directors for a school as an illustration. When a school has a special need, the directors will call a meeting; however, the general affairs of the school are usually taken care of by the principal and teachers. In Protestantism, the pastors and preachers are comparable to the principal and teachers of a school, and the elders and deacons are equivalent to directors of the board. However, this is not the revelation of the Bible. The Head has given gifts to the church, but these gifts should not replace the saints in the service. Hence, the co-workers must see clearly before the Lord that they should not serve in place of the saints.

This is the principle. The service of the co-workers in the churches should not replace the service of the saints. The Head gave gifts to the church, but His intention is not for them to replace the saints. Rather, His intention is for the gifts to work in the church to the extent that all the saints in the church can rise up to serve. The gifts should not replace the saints but rather perfect the saints so that each one can carry out his function. We need to see in this portion of the Word that Christ, the Head, gives gifts to build up the church by perfecting the saints so that those who do not know how to serve may learn to serve and those who do not know how to work may learn to work. This is the reason Ephesians 4:12 says, "For the perfecting of the saints unto the work of the ministry, unto the building up of the Body of Christ." This verse includes the work of the gifts and the issue of the believers carrying out the work of the ministry; it also includes the purpose for the perfecting of the saints by the gifts and the fruit of the saints' carrying out of the work of the ministry. The result of these two levels of service is the Body of Christ.

The work of the gifts is to perfect the saints. In the end, some saints may become elders and some may become deacons as a part of the perfecting work carried out by the gifts. Those who are sent directly by the Lord are the gifts spoken of in verse 11. These apostles, prophets, evangelists, and shepherds and teachers work in the church for the perfecting of the saints so that each one will be able to do the work of the ministry. For example, the work of the evangelists is to gain believers as building material for the church. After the material is obtained, the shepherds and teachers need to do the work of shepherding and teaching so that the material can be useful, that is, so that the believers can serve in the church. Therefore, the gifts are joined together in coordination to perfect the saints so that each saint can do the work of the ministry. After the believers are perfected and have grown in life, those who can serve as elders will be appointed elders, and those who care for the church affairs and love to serve the saints will be appointed deacons. In this way, through the perfecting by the gifted ones, all the saints will do the work of the ministry, and in the end, the Body of Christ will be built up.

The building up of the Body of Christ is the result of a twofold work: the result of the work of the gifts and the result of the saints who have been perfected. The result of the work of the gifts may be considered indirect; the result of the saints who have been perfected is direct. The building of the Body of Christ requires the work of the gifts on one hand and the saints doing the work of the ministry on the other hand. The result of the work of these two added together is the Body of Christ. Christ, the Head, gives gifts to the church, and these gifts then perfect the saints in the church to bring out their function, each doing the work of the ministry unto the building of the Body of Christ. As far as the building of the Body of Christ is concerned, the work of the gifts is indirect, but the work of the saints is direct.

THE GIFTS NOT REPLACING THE SAINTS IN THE SERVICE

Those who are truly called to work for the Lord should not replace the saints in the service. They should only perfect the saints, not replace them. All the elders and deacons should serve God directly; they should not serve in a way that they are replaced by others. They should build up the Body of Christ directly. Those who are workers, the gifts, do the work of perfecting the elders, the deacons, and the saints so that they might learn to serve, each one doing the work of the ministry for the building up of the Body of Christ. For the building up of the Body of Christ, the work of the gifts is not direct but indirect; it is the elders, deacons, and saints who build up the Body of Christ directly, resulting in the Body's building up of itself in love (v. 16). This portion of Ephesians, which begins with 4:11, does not end until the period at the end of verse 16. This implies that the meaning conveyed in this portion is not complete until the end of verse 16.

When co-workers are sent to work in different places, they must know that the service rendered to God in the church is the responsibility of the saints. The co-workers are sent by God to do the perfecting work so that the saints will be enabled and willing to serve. This will cause their service to be weighty for the building up of the Body of Christ, and in the end, this will cause the Body to build itself up in love. The apostles, prophets, evangelists, and shepherds and teachers do not build up the Body of Christ directly; the Body builds itself up directly in love.

When a certain church desires to go on, the saints in that locality may ask some co-workers to come and help. However, we should all be clear inwardly that the co-workers should not be substitutes for the serving ones; instead, they should perfect the saints for the service. This makes a great difference. All those who are blessed and who stand in the position of workers must see that they cannot replace the saints in serving God. Serving God is the responsibility of the saints; the workers called by the Lord should teach and perfect the saints so that those who do not know how to serve will learn to serve, so that those who are not willing to serve will be willing to serve, and so that those who do not take part in the service will bear a part in the service. After the gifted ones accomplish this work, the service of the church in that locality should be the responsibility of the saints; it must be the saints themselves who build up the church in their locality.

We must all be clear that those who administrate and serve the church are the elders and deacons. They should not expect co-workers to serve in their place. For example, if there is a center of work in the southern part of Taiwan and several co-workers go to help, the brothers in the south should not feel that they can be relieved because some are coming to bear the burden. If we have such an expectation, this shows that we do not know what it means to administrate the church. In the summer of 1946, I went to the southern part of Kiangsu province. When I first ministered the word in Nanking, I made it very clear to the brothers that they should not think that they were relieved of bearing any burden because I was there. I told them that I had come to unload many burdens onto them and that the more I worked, the more their burdens would increase. I was sent not to bear the burden for the brothers or to lessen their burden; instead, I went to give them more burdens.

The elders and deacons should not think that their burdens can be unloaded onto the co-workers who come into their midst. If there are one hundred and six pounds of burden in the church in Kaohsiung, the burden should be increased to one hundred and sixty pounds when the co-workers go and stay for two months. If this is not the case, we are not yet clear concerning our way. We need to be clear that those who directly serve the church are the saints in the church, including the elders and deacons. Gifts, when they are sent to various churches, should not serve in place of the saints; rather, they should perfect the saints to serve so that everyone will do the work of the ministry to build up the Body of Christ directly. The building up of the Body of Christ surely includes the work of the gifts, but more importantly, it is accomplished through the direct building of the saints. We should never think that the workers can serve in place of the local saints.

In the church, the elders should do what pertains to elders, and the deacons should do what pertains to deacons; the co-workers should never serve in place of the elders and deacons. The co-workers are commissioned only to perfect the elders, deacons, and saints so that they may rise up and serve. If we are sent to perfect others for the service, we should only perfect them and never replace them. If we are elders or deacons, we should never expect any workers to replace us in the service; rather, we must be perfected to rise up and serve. We must all be clear on this matter and firmly grasp this principle.

ARRIVING AT THE ONENESS OF THE FAITH
AND OF THE FULL KNOWLEDGE OF THE SON OF GOD

Ephesians 4:13 says, "Until we all arrive at the oneness of the faith and of the full knowledge of the Son of God,... at the measure of the stature of the fullness of Christ." Here it speaks of the work of the gifts on the saints; they perfect the saints until they all arrive at the oneness of the faith and of the full knowledge of the Son of God. *Faith* here is not a verb but a noun, denoting an object as an aim. The purpose of perfecting the saints is that they may arrive at the oneness of the faith and of the full knowledge of the Son of God; this is a great word. There is no oneness in today's Christianity. There are Presbyterian denominations, Baptist denominations, Seventh-day Adventists denominations, Lutheran denominations, Evangelical Lutheran denominations, and so forth, but there is no oneness. Although many say that their denominations are based upon the faith, the differences among the denominations in Christianity today are due to differences in their beliefs.

The Word, however, speaks of the saints being perfected until they all arrive at the oneness of the faith. Are the various denominations in Christianity today one in the faith? Some believe in baptism by immersion, and others believe in baptism by sprinkling; some believe in meeting on the Lord's Day, and others believe in meeting on Saturday. There are many such distinctions. How can they all arrive at the oneness of the faith? A brother may read from the Bible that it is more reasonable to meet on Saturday, the Sabbath, than on the Lord's Day, so he stresses this matter in his fellowship. Another brother may say that since the Bible refers to the Lord's Day, the believers in the New Testament should meet on the Lord's Day. If these two brothers quarrel, they will eventually split up into two parties, one holding a view concerning meeting on the Lord's Day and the other holding a view concerning meeting on Saturday. How can we arrive at the oneness of the faith? It all depends on the way we define *the faith.*

In Ephesians 4:13 Paul speaks of the need for all to arrive at the oneness of the faith, not only in relation to the saints but also in relation to the gifts in verse 11. The gifts also all need to arrive at the oneness of the full knowledge of the Son of God; then we will arrive at a full-grown man. If the light we receive stays merely on the surface of the truth, we will have no way to arrive at the oneness of the faith. It is only in the Son of God that we can arrive at the oneness of the faith. If we truly know the Son of God inwardly, whether we keep the Lord's Day or the Sabbath Day will not matter to us. Romans 14:5 says, "One judges one day above another; another judges every day alike. Let each be fully persuaded in his own mind." The Jews asked the Lord Jesus about the matter of profaning the Sabbath, and the Lord replied, "The Son of Man is Lord of the Sabbath" (Matt. 12:8). Actually, it is not a matter of the Sabbath but a matter of the *Lord.*

In order to administrate the church, the brothers must see Christ. Only when we take Christ as the center and focus on Him can we arrive at the oneness of the faith. Only in the Son of God can our faith be one. Once we deviate from this center, the oneness is gone. The more we firmly hold to the center—Christ, the Son of God—the fewer problems we will have; however, if we lose the center, we will have problems. Consider a wheel, for example. If we look at the hub, we see only one point, but if we look from the rim, we see many points. If we truly know the Son of God, there will be no arguments. This knowing does not depend on mental comprehension but on growth in life; this knowing is not in the mind but in experience. Hence, Ephesians 4:13 continues, saying, "At a full-grown man, at the measure of the stature of the fullness of Christ." From this verse we can see that knowing is the result of arriving at a full-grown man, at the measure of the stature of the fullness of Christ.

In 1935 when I was in Chefoo, I met a brother who was meeting in a place in the eastern part of Shantung province. The meeting was very good, but that year some problems arose. One brother thought that all the believers had to pass through the great tribulation before they could be raptured; however, another said that the rapture would occur before the great tribulation. This caused an argument. Some supported the thought of being raptured before the tribulation, and others supported the thought of being raptured after the tribulation. Originally there were about fifty to sixty people in their meeting, but toward the end of their time of arguing, less than ten were meeting. Consequently, some of them came to me for fellowship. I told them that if our argument did not enable others to know Christ, we should put this argument off to the future. Even though we may win an argument regarding the rapture, what is the profit if people do not know Christ? If we know and experience the Son of God, the matter of the prophecy regarding the rapture will not matter to us. The oneness of the faith among the saints does not depend on the rapture; rather, it depends on the Son of God, Christ.

In the matter of the administration and management of the church, the brothers must firmly grasp this point: Any practice that is not in contradiction to the Son of God, Christ, is acceptable. If we have seen this great principle, we will not have any arguments. The reason we argue is that we have not adequately seen this great principle. For instance, when the brothers speak of a certain problem, some insist that there is the need to deal with it, and others assert that seeing it is enough. If we take Christ—the Son of God—as the criterion and broaden our view, there will be no problem. All of our problems are due to our inadequate knowledge and vision of the Son of God. For example, as I am standing here, the front view of my face shows that I have a mouth, a nose, two eyes, and two ears, but the rear view shows nothing. If one person looks at me only from the front and another looks at me only from the back, they will have endless arguments regarding what I look like. This is because they have an incomplete seeing of me. All of our arguments are due to our inadequate seeing of the Son of God. The Sabbath is not simply a matter of the Sabbath but a matter based on what we have seen of the Son of God. If we know who the Son of God is and what His life is, this matter will be solved. It is the same with arguments over baptism by immersion. The more we see the Son of God, the more we will be clear as to whether or not we need to be baptized by immersion. Everyone who has truly seen the Son of God will not hold on to his opinion or insist on anything.

It is the same with the matter of head covering for the sisters. If the sisters truly know the Son of God, they will spontaneously cover their heads when they pray, without anyone giving a message on head covering. From our experience we know that exhorting the sisters to cover their head does not work, even if the brothers quote from 1 Corinthians to show that a sister needs to cover her head in order to be submissive. Even if this resulted in the sisters wearing a head covering, the head covering would be meaningless. But if a sister truly sees the Son of God and truly touches the Lord of glory, she will cover her head without the brothers' speaking concerning head covering. The oneness of the faith altogether depends on our full knowledge of the Son of God.

Suppose we are very clear that the church is the church and that there should not be any designation for the church, such as the Lutheran Church, Wesleyan Church, Presbyterian

Church, Baptist Church, Seventh-day Adventist Church, and so forth, because no church can be greater than Christ. If we meet someone who is a Wesleyan and tell him, "The church cannot denominate herself by any name," will our exhortation cause him to be one with us? No. Even if he tried to be one because of our exhortation, this oneness would be of no value. Sometimes speaking like this may even lead to a worse result; that is, we may argue with him and cause him to have a negative feeling toward us. This will produce nothing of value.

How can we arrive at the oneness of the faith and of the full knowledge of the Son of God? If we know the Lord of glory adequately and give Him enough ground in us, we will be full of Christ, the Son of God, when we come together with the brother who is a Wesleyan. Then we will not speak concerning the Wesleyan denomination, and we will also not spend time to speak concerning other denominations; rather, we will fellowship about the precious Christ whom we have seen and who is in us as the hope of glory. When we share in this way with him, the Wesleyan denomination will not be an issue with him. There will be no need for us to exhort him to forsake the Wesleyan denomination; he will forsake it himself. We can spontaneously bring people to know the Son of God because of our knowledge of the Son of God

We must see the center and must focus on the center. When we are at the center, there is no need to talk about oneness; we are spontaneously one with others. Baptism by immersion is not our opinion, head covering is not our doctrine, and being delivered from denominations is not our creed; our unique center is the Son of God—Christ. To arrive at the oneness of the faith is to arrive at the oneness of the full knowledge of the Son of God. In this way, we will arrive at a full-grown man experientially, at the measure of the stature of the fullness of Christ.

BEING ABLE TO ADMINISTRATE THE CHURCH BY KNOWING THE SON OF GOD

We must firmly grasp one thing, that is, we must take the knowledge of the Son of God as the center in our service to God. This is the same in our personal pursuit, and we also need to lead others to pay attention to this and know this. If we take care of this, we will have no base to argue with others. If a brother who holds a view that baptism by immersion is unnecessary and that baptism by sprinkling is good enough, what should we do? This is a matter of the administration of the church. If we reply, "We should bring this matter before the Lord," our answer is too general. If, however, we only explain the significance of baptism by immersion to him, this may provide him with some points, but it will not touch the principle of leading him to know the Son of God. All opinions and debates are an outward cloak; the real issue is that we do not have an adequate knowledge of the Son of God.

We all have to admit that we do not have an adequate knowledge of the Son of God. All opinions, views, and ideas are due to an insufficient knowledge of the Son of God. If a sister maintains that she does not need to cover her head, we should never argue with her, because it is useless. From her word and spirit, we can sense that she is full of the self and does not know what it means to have the Son of God in her as life or what it means to give herself to the Son of God. But when she is willing to give herself to the Son of God, she will spontaneously cover her head when she prays; there will be no need for any exhortation from others. The Son of God is the answer to all the problems.

If a quarreling couple comes to us, what should we do? It is better not to touch right or wrong. We must see that this couple will not quarrel if they have a further knowledge of the Son of God. Hence, we do not need to exhort the husband or the wife, because this is futile. We should help them know Christ, the Son of God, who is life in them. The Son of God is the answer and solution to every problem. All of our problems are due to not having an adequate knowledge of the Son of God.

Therefore, in order to administrate the church, we must know the Son of God and be filled with Him until we all arrive at the measure of the stature of the fullness of Christ. If this is the case, the Christ in us will be the way, the means, and the principle in our administration of the church. How we administrate the church depends on our knowledge of the Son of God. One who does not know Christ, the Son of God, can hardly lead others to know Christ, the Son of God. If we cannot lead the saints to this center, we will have no way to administrate the church well.

If two brothers come to us, arguing over the Lord's Day and the Sabbath, what should we do? What will happen if we say that according to doctrine the Lord's Day is right and the Sabbath is wrong? If we administrate the church and handle the matters among the saints in this way, not only will Christ, the Son of God, be gone, but the spirit and life of the church will also be gone. If we truly know the Son of God, we will stand between these two brothers and bring them out of the extremes of their insistence back to the center—Christ. We must lead them to know the Son of God; this is where we find the reality of the church, the content of the church.

The basic requirement for the administration of the church is knowledge of the Son of God, Christ. If the saints have not arrived at the oneness of the faith, they will have different views sooner or later. How should we carry out the administration of the church when different views appear? Should we discuss their views? Should we give them teachings? This is not the proper way to administrate the church. The only way is to know Christ.

The matter of knowing Christ is not something that can happen all at once; instead, we need to learn to know Christ, the Son of God, in a normal way. The apostle Paul said, "Until we all arrive at the oneness of the faith and of the full knowledge of the Son of God" (Eph. 4:13). This means that he could help others because he had arrived at this matter though practice.

According to 1 Corinthians, there were disputes and problems in the church in Corinth. Some of the Corinthians were focused on signs, and some on wisdom (1:22), yet Paul said, "But we preach Christ crucified" (v. 23). It seemed that the believers in Corinth knew everything, but Paul knew only Christ, and this One crucified (2:2). In 13:1 Paul said that without Christ, the Corinthian believers were but sounding brass and a clanging cymbal. Paul answered all of their questions with Christ and the cross. He reasoned with them, and he also spoke of resurrection (ch. 15). Regarding their erroneous doctrines, he dealt with them according to the truth. However, he solved the problems in the church by Christ, not by doctrines. This is a great principle. Our problem lies in our inadequate knowledge and experience of Christ. The administration of the church can be carried out only in the knowledge and experience of Christ.

Chapter Four

THE BUILDING AND THE ADMINISTRATION OF THE CHURCH

(2)

DISCERNING THE WINDS OF TEACHING

Scripture Reading: Eph. 4:12-14

THE ORDER IN EPHESIANS 4:12

Ephesians 4:11-12 shows that the service in the church is by gifts who perfect the saints so that they may carry out the ministry to build up the Body of Christ. This is a clear picture with a good order. Those who are gifts do not build up the Body of Christ directly; rather, they perfect the saints so that each one may do his part of the work of the ministry for the building up of the Body of Christ. We must grasp this order: at the top there is the Head of the Body who gives gifts for the edification and perfection of the saints so that everyone may do his part in the work of the ministry to build up the Body of Christ. This order involves the Head, the gifts, the saints, and the Body of Christ. This order enables us to clearly understand our position and our work.

ARRIVING IN EPHESIANS 4:13

Those who do the work of the ministry in the church include the elders, deacons, and serving ones. Their service is to bring all the saints to the oneness of the faith and of the full knowledge of the Son of God, with the result that we all arrive at a full-grown man and at the measure of the stature of the fullness of Christ (v. 13). When we carry out the work of the ministry in our service in the church, the stature of Christ, which is Christ Himself, will increase.

KNOWING THE SON OF GOD AND GROWING UP UNTO THE MEASURE OF THE STATURE OF CHRIST

Ephesians 4:13 says, "Until we all arrive at the oneness of the faith and of the full knowledge of the Son of God,...at the measure of the stature of the fullness of Christ." To arrive at the oneness of the faith is to arrive at the oneness of the full knowledge of the Son of God. However, Paul first speaks of the knowledge of *the Son of God,* and then he speaks of the measure of the stature of *Christ,* not of *the Son of God.* What is the difference between *the Son of God* and *Christ?* In terms of His person, the Lord Jesus is the Son of God; in terms of His work, He is Christ. The One we know is the Son of God, the life of God, and in the end we grow up unto the measure of the stature of Christ. In us there is the life of God, and on us there is the work of God. *Son of God* emphasizes the fact that God's life has entered into us; *Christ* refers to the fact that we have God's work on us. God's work is Christ Himself; Christ's work is for God to work Himself into us. The One we know is the Son of God, but eventually the issue of our growth is Christ.

We need to have the realization in the Holy Spirit that *the Son of God* always denotes God's life, and *Christ* denotes God's work. Since *the Son of God* denotes God's life, it denotes God's nature; since *Christ* denotes God's work, it denotes God's plan. In the church God wants the saints to grow up unto the measure of the stature of Christ by knowing the Son of God. This implies that God's life and nature are in the saints; at the same time, God's work and plan are also upon the saints. In other words, the saints have God's life and nature within them as a result of the accomplished work of Christ upon them.

Our service in the church should cause the saints to know the Son of God, to know the life and nature of God in His Son, that is, to know the life and nature of God Himself. A newly saved brother may only know that he has peace and joy; he may not know that God's life is in him. Through our service and fellowship, he should realize that he has the life and nature of the Son of God within him. First John 5:12 says that he who has the Son of God has the life; the eternal life is in the Son of God. When we speak of the Son of God, we touch

God's life and God's nature; God's life and nature are in the Son of God.

Our service in the church is to lead the brothers and sisters to touch God's life and nature and thereby allow God's plan to work in them. The result of the work of God's plan in us is the increase of Christ. When Christ increases in us, the stature of Christ will increase in us. For example, if a newly saved brother lives in the life of the Son of God, God's plan will work inwardly and cause the element of Christ to increase in him. The measure of the stature of Christ also will increase. This is the goal we must focus on and arrive at while we are administrating the church and ministering to the saints in our service to carry out the work of the ministry.

PAYING ATTENTION TO THE MATERIAL WE USE IN OUR SERVICE AND PREACHING ONLY CHRIST

Our service in the church is to lead the brothers and sisters to know the Son of God with the view that Christ will increase in them and that eventually they will arrive at the measure of the stature of the fullness of Christ. In order to arrive at such a goal, we need to pay attention to the material we use. The material that we use in order to cause people to know the Son of God and have the measure of the stature of the fullness of Christ is a very important matter. For example, when a chair is made, we must pay attention to the material we use in addition to knowing size and quantity. The material we use must be the Son of God, Christ. We can cause the saints to know the Son of God only by using the Son of God as the material. We can cause the increase of Christ in the saints only by using Christ as the material. Our preaching alone will not necessarily cause the saints to know the Son of God. In order for the saints to know the Son of God, we must use the Son of God as the material; in order for the saints to have the increase of Christ in them, we must use Christ as the material.

If we preach the Bible with the teachings of Confucius and Mencius, can we cause people to know the Son of God or have the increase of Christ? We can cause people to know the Son of God only when our preaching and our utterance and eloquence are the Son of God. We cannot be loose in this matter; rather, we must grasp it firmly. A sister once told me that I should give messages on husbands loving their wives and wives submitting to their husbands, because she thought that it would be difficult for people to come into the church without such messages. Frankly speaking, if I gave messages on honoring parents, submitting to husbands, and loving wives, I could move many people to tears. However, I have not been sent to give this kind of message or to reform people's ethics. Such messages do not cause people to have more Christ. I am not a servant of ethics; I am a slave of Christ.

Someone also wrote to me anonymously and asked me to speak concerning heaven and hell. Actually, it is much easier to speak concerning heaven and hell than to speak concerning Christ and the cross. I could speak concerning hell for eight or ten days and concerning heaven for another eight or ten days. I could incite tremendous fear in people when speaking concerning hell, and I could stir up a strong yearning when speaking concerning heaven. However, I have not been sent to speak concerning heaven or hell; rather, I have seen the Lord of glory, and I have been sent by Him. I am filled with Him, and all of my inward feeling is toward Him.

TAKING CHRIST AS THE MATERIAL

One message may differ from another message, and not every message can cause the element of Christ to increase in people. Only Christ Himself can cause people to know Christ and have Christ increase in them. If we speak to people about loving their wives, submitting to their husbands, honoring their parents, and nurturing their children, we must speak Christ into them as their love, submission, honoring, and nurturing. When a sister submits to her husband, her submission must be Christ. By loving Christ, being filled with Christ, fellowshipping with Christ, and allowing Christ to live in her and out of her, she will experience the reality of submission. This also applies to husbands; the love with which they love their wives must come from the dispensing of Christ into them. Those who fellowship with Christ and allow Christ to live in them surely will respect, love, and be considerate of their wives. The care of parents for their children should be so spiritual that it is evident that their care is Christ. Hence, the love with which husbands love their wives is Christ; a parent's love, teaching, and care for their children should also be Christ. All of these virtues should come out of Christ. If we are filled with Christ inwardly, how can we not take care of our children? How could we not honor and be considerate of our parents? This care, honoring, and considerateness are just Christ Himself.

Our church life must be so strong that a husband's love for his wife should enable others to see Christ, a wife's submission should enable others to see Christ, and a child's considerateness and honor toward his parents should enable others to see Christ. If everything is filled with Christ, then whether we are speaking about filial piety, love, or submission, others can gain Christ. It is only when we take the Son of God as the material that we can cause others to know the Son of God and to gain the Son of God. Only when we take Christ as the material can we cause others to gain Christ and know Christ.

To speak of taking Christ as the material is easy, but taking Christ as the material requires experience in practice. If we deal with our wives and husbands apart from Christ and have never learned this lesson, we will not be able to take Christ as the material. If we have learned the lesson of knowing and experiencing Christ in dealing with our wives, we will spontaneously take Christ as the material when we contact people. If we truly know the inward life of the Son of God, live in this life, take this life in dealing with our wives and husbands, and live with our wives and husbands according to this life, we will be able to fellowship with people who are encountering difficulties in dealing with their wives and husbands. Only in this way will our work have spiritual value and be effective. Otherwise, our work will bear the name of Christ, but in reality it will be only a religious work. In other words, our work will be in the name of Christ but without the reality of Christ. We must speak in the name of Christ, speak the word of Christ, and speak Christ into others.

THE FOUNDATION OF OUR PREACHING BEING CHRIST

Someone may ask, "Why do some co-workers teach people not to wear fashionable clothing, put on lipstick, or go to the movies?" If we merely focus on whether it is right to put on lipstick or wear fashionable clothing, at the most we are preachers who can improve society. In teaching people not to do things, such as going to movies, wearing fashionable clothing, or giving a permanent wave to their hair, we must have Christ as the firm foundation. Only when we teach from Christ as the foundation can there be any true value and impact. We cannot wear fashionable clothing because Christ is in us; we cannot go to the movies because Christ is in us. Not wearing fashionable clothing and not going to the movies must come from Christ. If it does not come from Christ, it does not make any difference whether we wear a fancy dress or a plain dress. Our preaching must convey nothing other than Christ Himself. We preach Christ to build up, edify, and perfect the saints. The material with which we build up, edify, and perfect others is Christ Himself. Every message should be centered on Christ; every exhortation must be joined to Christ and take Christ as the foundation. Our exhortations must bring people into Christ.

We are not here to study doctrinal questions. Neither are we here to learn how to preach from the podium, to learn how to converse with people, or to learn how to serve in the church; all of these things are just technical matters. Basically, we must know Christ, experience Christ, and gain Christ inwardly. In this way, we will be able to minister and dispense Christ when the need arises. Then we can supply others with the Christ whom we know and experience by applying the techniques of speaking and the methods of work that we have learned.

BEING NO LONGER LITTLE CHILDREN
CARRIED ABOUT BY THE WINDS OF TEACHING

Ephesians 4:14 says, "That we may be no longer little children...carried about by every wind of teaching in the sleight of men, in craftiness with a view to a system of error." This is a word on the negative side. On one hand, we need to arrive at the full-grown man spoken of in verse 13; on the other hand, as verse 14 says, we should no longer be little children. To be little children is a spiritual rather than a physical matter. We need to be *like* little children (cf. Matt. 18:3; Mark 10:15; Luke 18:17), but we should not *be* little children. After many years some people are still little children who have not grown up. Being little children indicates the lack of growth in life. Being a little child puts one at risk to easily fall into the schemes of men and to be deceived. A little child can be deceived by a piece of chocolate. Some brothers and sisters are lured away merely by a good meeting or a good teaching. Little children easily fall into the schemes of men.

If we could ask the apostle Paul to come and speak of things that could inspire little children, he would say that such things are of the flesh. Sometimes after hearing a good message by someone in a certain place, some brothers have asked me if we should invite him to come and speak to us. I usually do not reply to them because I realize that they are like little children speaking nonsensical words. There are some brothers and sisters who spoke such nonsensical words four or five years ago who still speak such words. We truly need the Lord's mercy to no longer be little children. Since little children neither know nor understand what they should do, they are easily deceived.

THE WINDS OF TEACHING
CARRYING PEOPLE AWAY FROM CHRIST

In our service in the church, the way is Christ, and the material also is Christ. Ephesians 4:14 says that there are all kinds of winds of teaching, like storms, hurricanes, or strong gales. There are all kinds of winds coming from the pulpits in Christianity. An elderly brother, who paid much attention to morality, once quoted twenty-eight portions from Exodus to Ephesians and spoke an attractive message about honoring parents. Upon hearing him, many university students were touched; they felt that God had shone a great light. From the human perspective, this message helped people to honor their parents; however, from the perspective of Christ, it was a wind of teaching that carried people to another place. This does not mean that we should not speak of honoring parents; rather, our honoring of parents should be Christ. If we merely teach people to honor their parents without bringing Christ to them and imparting Christ into them, our teaching will only be like the teaching of Confucius or Mencius. The essence and content of all the teachings in the Bible, including honoring parents, loving wives, or submitting to husbands, are just Christ.

If the sisters are all filled with Christ and are submissive to their husbands as a result of our preaching of submission, then this preaching is the preaching of Christ, not a wind of teaching that carries people away from Christ. Today there are countless winds of teaching coming from the pulpits of Christianity, carrying people away from Christ. Our preaching of the gospel is to bring people to Christ, but it is a sad thing if a person is carried away from Christ by the winds of teaching after he is saved. Some teachings are based on the Scriptures, but their essence is not Christ; some teachings are good from the human perspective, but their content is not Christ. No matter what we preach, we should take Christ as the center and remain with Christ, taking Him as the essence and content.

Even if our preaching is on matters related to our daily living, such as how to dress properly, it still must be according to Christ. In this way, after someone hears such a message, he will kneel down before the Lord and say, "O Lord, thank You for teaching me how to dress properly." Only this kind of preaching is genuine and scriptural. Instead of carrying people away from Christ, this kind of preaching brings people into Christ. Otherwise, no matter how good a teaching may be, it can be a wind that carries us away from Christ. Although it is a good teaching, it is a wind that carries people away from Christ.

Every message, regardless of its topic, should cause people to desire Christ and desire to submit to Christ, thereby bringing them into Christ. Whether it is a message on loving one's wife, on submitting to one's husband, or on wearing proper clothing, the effect should be that the more a person listens, the more he loves Christ, desires Christ, and is filled with

Christ. If this is not the case, no matter how appealing and inspiring the message may be, it will be a wind of teaching that carries people away from Christ. It would be better if people did not listen to the message, because they were closer to Christ before hearing the message. After listening to the message, they may be headed in the direction of something good, but they are further and further away from the goal—Christ. This is to be carried about by the wind.

A brother may give a message concerning music, and we will all be burdened to learn how to sing hymns and practice our singing skills, but in the end we may not know or gain more of Christ. This kind of message is a wind of teaching which carries us away from Christ. Another brother may come and give a series of messages on the significance of numbers in the Bible. He may speak concerning the number six hundred sixty-six and the seventy weeks, and then, for a period of two years, we may have hardly any fellowship with Christ because we are spending all our time studying these numbers. We may be very clear on the significance of the seventy weeks in the book of Daniel—we may be able to recite it, draw a chart, tell people when King Nebuchadnezzar was dethroned, when his kingship was restored, when Daniel was harmed, when Jerusalem was rebuilt, and when the seventy weeks will begin—yet we may not have drawn any nearer to Christ. This is to be carried away from Christ by a wind of teaching. Even though we have not committed any sin and, instead, have studied only the seventy weeks and the number six hundred sixty-six, finding all the related verses in the Bible, we have not focused on Christ, and we have missed Christ.

SATAN'S SYSTEM OF ERROR

The full-grown men in Ephesians 4:13 do not listen to winds of teaching, because they are aware of this deception. When they hear messages concerning the seventy weeks and the number six hundred sixty-six, they know that the Bible is being used as a front to deceive people. Because of their knowledge of the Son of God, they are full-grown men and have the measure of the stature of Christ. They are not affected by winds of teaching, and they are not tossed or carried about by them. The winds of teaching are in the sleight of men, in craftiness with a view to a system of error (v. 14); hence, it is a system of error. All those who know spiritual warfare admit that this refers to Satan's craftiness in the church. These winds of teaching come from the satanic system. The messages that often appeal to and inspire men are actually part of Satan's plot.

If someone among us teaches us not to honor our parents, we surely would not listen to him because we are convinced that that is from Satan. However, if we deviate from Christ after hearing an appealing message concerning honoring our parents, this is still the craftiness of Satan. If someone teaches us not to read the Bible, we surely would not listen to him. However, if someone says that the Bible is truly wonderful because it contains such matters as the number six hundred sixty-six and the seventy weeks, and if, by listening to him, we are carried away from Christ, then this kind of teaching is a scheme of the evil one. The scheme of Satan is a system of error deliberately arranged by him. Satan causes some to speak attractive messages in the church, and he uses these messages to carry believers away from Christ so that they will not know Christ as life, even though they have been saved for years.

I am afraid that there are many such ones among us; they may have been saved for more than ten years, and they listen to messages and attend meetings week after week, but they still do not know Christ as life in them. This is because the teachings they hear cause them to be carried away from Christ. A message may be scriptural, may be derived from the Bible, and may be said to be from God, but if this message does not stir us to love Christ, incline toward Christ, be filled with Christ, live in Christ, and live out Christ, then it is a wind of teaching that carries us away from Christ. This kind of message is a part of Satan's scheme to annul the work of the Holy Spirit. Today many seemingly proper teachings distract believers from Christ. These teachings apparently come from men as a result of their study, but they actually are the scheme of the evil one and belong to the system of the evil one. Through the winds of teaching, Satan carries believers away and leads them into his system of error. He is like a magician who causes people to be deceived by his sleight of hand without them even knowing it.

BEING WARY OF THE CRAFTINESS OF SATAN

Practically, we must consider whether our preaching of the word carries people away from Christ. Many brothers may not want to carry people away and are not purposely doing this, but in the end they still do it. If we do not have a thorough understanding of Satan's craftiness and are not wary of it, we may turn to our mind instead of our spirit when we are about to preach the word. Spontaneously, we will fall into Satan's system of error and yield to his maneuver and plot. For example, we may realize that we do not have the eloquence to preach Christ and the cross. Consequently, another topic, such as the number six hundred sixty-six and the seventy weeks, may suddenly come up in our mind, and so we think that we should speak about it in order to prove that the Bible is marvelous. When we preach according to the topic conceived in our mind, it may be very interesting, and the brothers and sisters may be touched and determined to study the Bible. However, unconsciously they will lose their focus on Christ, and their mind will be full of numbers.

Moreover, because one brother spoke concerning the number six hundred sixty-six and the seventy weeks, when another brother is about to speak, he also will consider what to speak in order to attract people. Should he speak concerning service in coordination? What if the saints do not respond? Should he speak concerning Christ as life? What if no one is touched? Should he speak concerning the termination of the old man by the cross of Christ? What if he is short of utterance? He does not know what he should speak. After considering for many days and after much prayer, he feels that he should avoid the subject of Christ being our life. Instead, he chooses to tell a wonderful story regarding the experience of a certain spiritual giant. He presents it in a marvelous way so that many brothers and sisters are moved, but no one has touched Christ. A week later, another brother may be in the same situation. He considers a topic but rejects it as not being attractive, and he considers another topic, but rejects it as uninspiring. Instead, he gives a message on being good, which does not cause people to touch Christ. Thus, message after message are only winds of teaching that blow the brothers and sisters in one direction and then in another direction. After being blown for many years, they still do not know Christ or know how to live in Christ, and Christ's life in them has not increased.

Therefore, we must see through the craftiness of the devil. The enemy tries to use these schemes to systematically annul the work of the Holy Spirit to enable people to know the Son of God. We may have been Christians for many years, but do we realize that we must know Christ inwardly, be filled with Christ, and allow Christ to live in us? If the messages we hear do not help us in these points, they are but winds of teaching. This month we will be blown in the direction of being good, and next month we will be blown in the direction of studying the Bible. Although these messages may touch us and may be good, after ten or twenty years we still will not be any closer to Christ and to the knowledge of Christ as life, and Christ's life will not be increased in us. We will only have been tossed about by waves caused by the wind.

DISCERNING THE WINDS OF TEACHING AND EXPERIENCING CHRIST

Concerning the administration of the church, all of the co-workers, elders, deacons, and everyone who learns to serve God must look to the Lord for His mercy so that we may see how we should serve, with what we should serve, and the purpose of our service. We need to see the negative side as well as the positive side. Many elders and deacons speak message after message to the saints when they administrate and serve the church. However, the more they speak, the more the winds of teaching toss the saints. Since they do not have adequate inward knowledge, some brothers lead others away from Christ by their speaking, even when they are trying to help others. Hence, we must be careful not only in listening to messages but also in fellowshipping with others. If we are not careful, we will be unconsciously deceived by the evil one and carry people away by the messages we speak.

For this reason, we do not agree with putting out any publication that is written by those outside of us. This is because many so-called "good" books convey winds of teaching which carry the saints away from Christ. I hope that we all can pay more attention to the "wind of teaching" spoken of in Ephesians 4:14 so that when we go to a certain place and listen to the preaching, we will be able to tell whether it is a wind of teaching. When we speak with people, we should be cautious concerning whether we are blowing a wind of teaching. We can determine this by Ephesians 4:13, which says, "Until we all arrive at the oneness of the faith and of the full knowledge of the Son of God, at a full-grown man, at the measure of the stature of the fullness of Christ."

Our service in the church is to cause people to know the Son of God and to reach the measure of the stature of the fullness of Christ; hence, we should never use any substitute for Christ. We should take only the Son of God—Christ—as the material; then we will be able to generate and produce Christ. May God be merciful to us so that our eyes will be opened to see the administration of the church. All of the administration in the church should be Christ. Since the purpose of the administration of the church is for people to gain Christ, we should use only Christ as the material when we administrate the church. Therefore, we must know Christ, experience Christ, and gain Christ. When we have the experience of Christ in all things, we will be able to dispense Him and bring Him to others in our daily living.

Chapter Five

THE BUILDING AND THE ADMINISTRATION OF THE CHURCH

(3)

HOLDING TO TRUTH AND GROWING UP INTO CHRIST THE HEAD

Scripture Reading: Eph. 4:14-15; Col. 2:19

THE GOAL OF GOD'S PLAN AND SATAN'S NULLIFYING WORK

Ephesians 4:13 says, "Until we all arrive at the oneness of the faith and of the full knowledge of the Son of God, at a full-grown man, at the measure of the stature of the fullness of Christ." This means that we should enable the saints to know the Son of God to such an extent that the church may reach the measure of the stature of the fullness of Christ. We need to pay attention to the full knowledge of the Son of God and to the measure of the stature of the fullness of Christ in the church. This is the goal of God's eternal plan and the purpose of His work. Once His will is accomplished, God's purpose in the universe will be achieved. Hence, we should not pass by this point quickly. The full knowledge of the Son of God and arriving at the measure of the stature of the fullness of Christ in the church are great and high matters. We need to see this in our service to God in the church. This is the goal that God wants to attain in His creation and in the church from eternity to eternity.

In Ephesians 4:14 many distracting things are present, including Satan's craftiness, Satan's sleights, and Satan's system. Those who have the experience of spiritual warfare know the subtlety of Satan. In this verse, those who fall into Satan's craftiness are little children, those who are immature in life. If we are immature in the church, we will be deceived at some point in time. Satan's teaching is "in the sleight of men." Here *men* is used symbolically; in fact, the emphasis here is not on men but on God's adversary—Satan.

Verses 12 and 13 show how the Holy Spirit works through the gifts so that we can arrive at the measure of the stature of the fullness of Christ to fulfill God's eternal purpose, and verse 14 shows the nullifying work of Satan in the church. On one hand, there is God's building work; on the other hand, there is Satan's nullifying work. God is causing the stature of Christ to grow to its full measure in the church through the perfecting of the saints by the gifts, but Satan also has a system and scheme, and he is doing a nullifying work in the church. The purpose of his work is to bring people into a system of error. Thus, we should not consider the expressions in verse 14, including *sleight, craftiness,* and *system of error,* in a light way. Rather, we must give them much consideration. Only when we spend time to study these verses will we understand the meaning that the Holy Spirit intends to convey.

The work of Satan in the church comes from the system, arrangement, and purpose in his plot, which is to bring man into a system of error by sleight and craftiness. He carries out his evil plot by the winds of teaching. We must understand that winds of teaching have been greatly utilized by Satan in the church; this is a serious matter. Ephesians 4:12-13 reveals that God's work in the church is for man to know His Son and for the measure of the stature of the fullness of Christ to increase in the church; this is God's eternal goal. However, verse 14 shows that the crafty one, Satan, brings man into a system of error by craftiness and sleight through the winds of teaching. We must all see this point.

Christ is God's goal, the center of God's work. God desires to work Christ into man, and this kind of work is carried out through the cross. By God's grace, we have been doing this work. We must confess that this is not out of man's imagination or preference; instead, this is the Spirit's motivation among us.

Our burden is to show the saints that the perfecting of the saints in Ephesians 4:12 is for God's children to know Christ, the Son of God, and for the measure of the stature of the fullness of Christ to increase in the church. However, while we are serving in the churches, we may speak messages out from ourselves. This is the work of the evil one, the crafty one, according to his scheme and system. He puts many appealing messages into our mind so that even though the messages are interesting, inspiring, and captivating, they do not have Christ as the center and the life of the Son of God as the content. These messages are winds of teaching raised up by the sleight of Satan, which carry the saints away from Christ. In this way, the work of God can be completely nullified.

SATAN UTILIZING WINDS OF TEACHING

The greatest tool that Satan uses for his nullifying work in the church is the winds of teaching. Hence, we need to stand and guard against any wind of teaching. What is a wind of teaching? Any preaching that does not take Christ as the center and the Son of God as the content is a wind of teaching. Regardless of the verses that someone quotes in his preaching and even the scriptural basis for his teaching, if his preaching does not take Christ as the center and the Son of God as the content, it is a wind of teaching. The content of the Bible is Christ; Christ is the center of the Bible. If we remove Christ from the Bible, the Bible becomes empty. Today many people take a verse or a portion from the Bible and give message after message, but they have not taken the Bible as the content. They select material from the Bible, but they do not take the Bible as the content. Hence, they preach from the Bible in name but not in reality. Any preaching of the word that is genuinely from the Bible must take Christ as the center and the Son of God as the content. Otherwise, thousands of messages which claim to be scriptural will not be scriptural but in fact will be winds of teaching.

Any message that does not take Christ as the center, that does not take the Son of God as the content, that cannot bring man into Christ, and that cannot bring Christ into man is a wind of teaching. Ephesians 4:14 speaks of Satan's craftiness and sleight; he uses the winds of teaching as his tool. Everything that is done in craftiness is done in a fine and detailed way. Appealing messages in Christianity often are produced by Satan after a long period of consideration in order to fulfill his purpose. Satan fulfills his purpose by his system of error.

If we have seen this, we will not regard eloquence as the criterion when we listen to a message, and we will not admire attractive expressions, beautiful utterances, and inspiring power, because even though it may be an appealing message, it can be a trick used by Satan to deceive us. When we listen to a message or a testimony from the brothers and sisters, we need to take Christ as the center and the Son of God as the content and check whether the message or testimony causes us to touch Christ and be filled with Christ inwardly. If this is not the case, we should be aware that the appealing message is but the craftiness and sleight of Satan. If we can exercise such discernment, we are no longer little children.

NOT BEING CARRIED ABOUT
BY THE WINDS OF TEACHING

Someone may be a very eloquent speaker, moving others to tears even if he does not speak of God or Christ. Even though this kind of preaching may be inspiring, according to Ephesians 4:13-14, it is but the sleight of the evil one. Satan uses eloquent speaking to form winds of teaching that toss the saints and carry them away from Christ. Some may say that they are weeping because they love the Lord; however, loving the Lord is a matter of degree. Some may love the Lord for many years without knowing Christ as life and without living in Him. This kind of person can be easily touched when he listens to messages because of his inward affection. Regardless of the center or content of the messages, he is easily touched. If we speak concerning numbers in the Bible, such as the number six hundred sixty-six and the seventy weeks, he will be touched; if we speak concerning hymns, he will be touched also. These people are touched because of eloquence and utterance. Therefore, even though they love the Lord and are zealous in the church, they can still be tossed and carried away after ten or twenty years. Winds of teaching refer to messages that are seemingly pure and proper but do not take Christ as the center and the Son of God as the content.

We often hear saints testify of how the Lord answered their prayers by healing their sicknesses. This kind of experience is not bad, but it can be used by the evil one as a wind of teaching. Some among us have learned the lessons of prayer for many years, but they still do not know Christ as life. They only know that God answers their prayers, but they have not seen that the Son of God who answers their prayers is now living in them as life. They only see God who is on the throne and who is faithful and merciful. When they pray to Him according to His Word, that is, when they petition Him by the blood of His Son, God often answers their prayer. But they have not seen that the God who answers prayer is now in His Son and living in them as life. Whether God answers their prayers is not the most important matter; what is important is that God desires to work His Son into them so that they may have His life and nature and so that He may live in them.

In the Bible, neither Paul, Peter, nor John ever gave a testimony about how God answered their prayers. Rather, in Ephesians 1:17 Paul prayed, saying, "That the God of our Lord Jesus Christ, the Father of glory, may give to you a spirit of wisdom and revelation in the full knowledge of Him." In 3:16 through 19 he bowed his knees unto the Father, praying, "That He would grant you, according to the riches of His glory, to be strengthened with power through His Spirit into the inner man, that Christ may make His home in your hearts through faith, that you, being rooted and grounded in love, may be full of strength to apprehend with all the saints what the breadth and length and height and depth are and to know the knowledge-surpassing love of Christ, that you may be filled unto all the fullness of God."

The Lord clearly said that we should not be anxious for food, drink, or clothing, for all these things the Gentiles anxiously seek (Matt. 6:31-32). If a certain brother cannot find a house, he may pray, "O Lord, I do not want a house that is too big; it will be sufficient if it is about three hundred square feet. O Lord, please do not let your children have any lack."

He may pray again and again and even remember a verse in the Bible to firmly hold on to in his prayers. Two weeks later, after finding a place that is bigger than three hundred square feet, he will stand up and testify in the meeting. He will quote Psalm 23 and praise the Lord for being a good Shepherd to him because he lacks nothing. He will testify that those who seek Jehovah will not lack any good thing (34:10). Two months later when this brother loses his job, he will ask the church to pray for him, and he and his wife will fast and pray at home. A few days later after finding a good job, he will testify again about learning the lesson of prayer. God truly looks upon His children, but the things that the brother asks for are only the things that the Gentiles anxiously seek. The Lord wants us to seek first His kingdom and His righteousness (Matt. 6:33). What are His kingdom and His righteousness? We will know God's kingdom and God's righteousness only when we know that the Christ of God is the center and that the Son of God is the content.

The evil one can use all kinds of messages and testimonies as winds of teaching. Even something such as learning the lesson of prayer can be a wind of teaching. We may have had several experiences in which God answered our prayers, but we still may not know Christ as life or know that God's unique work is to work in us to the point that Christ is everything in us. This is God's unique goal. The evil one wants to nullify the work of God's eternal goal. If we have been a Christian for thirty years and have only learned the lesson of prayers being answered, but we do not have the experience of Christ living in us and being constituted in us, God has not accomplished His purpose in us.

As far as our prayer is concerned, God may have truly answered our prayer; however, as far as God's eternal purpose is concerned, there is no difference between us and an unbeliever. Just as God's eternal purpose cannot be fulfilled in an unbeliever, it cannot be fulfilled in those who have only learned the lesson of prayer. Just as an unbeliever does not know the life of Christ, we do not know the life of Christ. This is what the evil one does, and this is what Ephesians 4:14 reveals. Even things such as answered prayers can be something in Satan's system that shifts our focus. We may think that we have learned the lesson of prayer, without realizing that Satan has brought us into his system of error. Hence, we need to be careful not only in listening to messages but also in speaking. If we are not careful, what we speak can become a wind of teaching that distracts people from Christ.

Some saints truly love the Lord, and they know that the Lord's sweet desire is to live in them and be the Lord and King in them; hence, they are willing to take Him as everything and to give themselves to Him. This is not a matter of prayer or fervency but a matter of the "I" being lost in the Lord. When they love the Lord in such a way, they experience crucifixion with Christ. "It is no longer I who live, but it is Christ who lives in me" (Gal. 2:20). Because the Lord loved us and gave Himself up for us, we also love Him and give ourselves up for Him. His giving Himself up for us is by dying on the cross; our giving ourselves up for Him is by giving ourselves to Him. Only this kind of love is proper and fitting. How many in the church love the Lord in this way? Sometimes when preachers speak concerning loving the Lord, the message they give becomes a wind of teaching. Their original intention was to stir up the saints to love the Lord, but in the end they distract the saints from Christ, because they do not take Christ as the center when they exhort the saints to love the Lord. Instead, they take zeal, diligence, and serving the church as the center. Thus, the saints do not love Christ Himself. Even messages on love, zeal, diligence, meekness, and endurance can become winds of teaching which carry people away from Christ.

HOLDING TO TRUTH

Ephesians 4:15 says, "Holding to truth in love, we may grow up into Him in all things, who is the Head, Christ." After verse 14 speaks of the sleight of men, craftiness, and a system of error, verse 15 speaks of "holding to truth." Verse 15 says that we should hold to truth because the situation spoken of in verse 14 is not proper.

What is the truth? The truth is God being manifested in the flesh, God becoming flesh. To hold to truth is to hold to the matter of God being manifested in the flesh. If a brother's preaching is inspiring but does not cause people to touch Christ, we must refuse it regardless of its appeal. Holding to truth means that we want only one kind of preaching, which is God manifested in the flesh; this is holding to truth in love. In order to face the winds of teaching, we need to hold to truth, which is the manifestation of God in the flesh.

Someone once lent me a book about the restoration of the Jewish nation over a period of time in the land of Judea. When I first read this book, I felt that it was quite meaningful, but in fact, even this book has the danger of becoming a wind of teaching because I may not remain in fellowship with Christ by studying it. This does not involve heresy, but it can be utilized by Satan as a wind of teaching to blow people away and not hold to truth.

The word *truth* is used in the Old Testament but not as frequently as it is in the New Testament. In the New Testament *truth* does not refer merely to doctrine but to God becoming flesh. Truth is reality, which came through Jesus Christ (John 1:17). This incarnated One said, "I am...the reality" (14:6). The apostle John refers to truth the most. *Truth* in the Bible is a particular noun which specifically speaks of the matter of God becoming flesh. The Greek word for *truth* denotes reality, not doctrine. God is real; if God were taken away from the universe, everything would be vanity.

When a couple is getting married, they prepare a bridal chamber. If both the bridegroom and the bride are absent on the day of the wedding, the bridal chamber is vain. The reality of the bridal chamber lies in the bridegroom and the bride. Please remember that God is the reality of the universe; only the God who became flesh is *real*. An unsaved person lacks reality, but when he is saved and receives God into him, *reality* enters into him. Then he is full of reality. In like manner, today many saints are leading a life that is not real because they do not have *reality* in their living. Only God is real; holding to truth is not holding to the doctrines in the Bible but holding to the matter of God being manifested in the flesh. Strictly speaking, in the narrow sense, to hold to truth is to hold to the fact of God's manifestation in the flesh.

In the past when I came across books related to prophecy, I had the intention to study them, but I also inwardly realized that I should hold to truth. As a result, I forsook my intention. We should preach only Christ and the cross. "For indeed Jews require signs and Greeks seek wisdom, but we preach Christ crucified" (1 Cor. 1:22-23). Some preach signs, but we preach Christ; some preach wisdom, but we preach Christ crucified. If I was a revivalist, I could go to many places to speak revival messages, and many could be stirred up but still not touch Christ. Therefore, what would be the use of listening to such messages? We need to hold to truth and not fall into the craftiness and sleight of the evil one. We should not be led into a system of error or be carried away by winds of teaching. A wind of teaching may be a wholesome doctrine or even a scriptural doctrine, but it is not the truth, because it does not show people that the Son of God is in them as life and that Christ is in them as their everything.

HOLDING TO TRUTH IN LOVE

Ephesians 4:15 says, "Holding to truth in love." Truth is held in *love*. In the New Testament those who live before God must have love; those who only fear God cannot live before Him. A couple is married in love, not in fear. Couples who have been married for a long time look like each other in behavior and demeanor because they are in love.

Paul says, "He died for all that those who live may no longer live to themselves but to Him who died for them and has been raised" (2 Cor. 5:15). He also says, "It is no longer I who live, but it is Christ who lives in me...who loved me and gave Himself up for me" (Gal. 2:20). The Lord Jesus' word also indicates, "If anyone loves Me, he will keep My word, and My Father will love him, and We will come to him and make an abode with him" (John 14:23). At the end of the Gospel of John, the Lord asked Peter, "Do you love Me more than these?" (21:15), and then He asked him the second time and third time, "Do you love Me?" (vv. 16-17). From these verses we can see that holding to truth must be *in love*. We must say to God, "No matter where You place me, I do not fear; I hold to truth, not because of fear but because of love."

Song of Songs in the Old Testament is a book that begins with love, passes through love, and eventually arrives at love. In the beginning the seeker says, "Let him kiss me with the kisses of his mouth!" (1:2). If you love someone, this is the best way to express your love. If your wife loves you, she will not be herself; she will be you. If you love your wife, you will not be yourself; you will be her. Your being her and her being you is true love. The utmost love is not to be yourself but to be the one whom you love. Many couples who have been in love for decades are almost alike in their behavior and demeanor.

The Lord became flesh to be like us because He loves us. The highest expression of God's love toward us is His becoming a man to be us. God did not only remain as God; He came to be a man. This is incarnation. This can be compared to a husband who no longer remains as a husband only; he also becomes the wife. If a husband only regards his position, this shows that he does not love his wife at all. One who truly loves his wife is willing to forsake his status as the husband in order to accommodate his wife. When people see him, they will wonder if he is the husband or the wife. This is the story of the incarnated Jesus, the Nazarene. Is He God or a man? He became a man to be us because He loves us to the uttermost. Conversely, when we love Him to the uttermost, we also should be like Him. From the side of the wife, we should become the husband; from the side of the husband, we should become the wife. Although we may not be exactly alike, we should at least be half alike. God came from heaven; the Word became flesh to be like us. If we want to respond to His love, the flesh must become the Word; we should no longer be man but be God.

Christians should be like Christ; we who love God should be like God. At the end of the Song of Songs, the Shulammite and Solomon are like each other, and they are in a union of love which is as strong as death (8:6). Thus, when their love for each other reaches the peak, Solomon is like the Shulammite, and the Shulammite is like Solomon; this means that God is like man, and man is like God (1 John 3:2). When the love of the two parties reaches the climax, their union in love is as strong as death. We need to hold to truth in such a love.

GROWING UP INTO THE HEAD IN ALL THINGS

When we hold to truth in love, the result will be that we grow up into Him in all things, who is the Head, Christ (Eph. 4:15). God loves us and wants to be like us; we love God and want to be like God. Truth is God becoming man, and truth is also man becoming God. In love we hold to the truth so that He becomes us, and we become Him. He loves us, and we love Him. In this way, we will grow up into Him in all things; this means that we will grow up into the Head, Christ, in all things. How sweet this is!

When we grow up into Him in all things, who is the Head, Christ, the result is that everything we do will come out of Christ the Head and will be Him. We love our Lord in the way He loved us by becoming flesh. The result of our holding to truth in love is that we grow up into the Head, Christ.

Our dealings with the brothers and sisters may be natural and may come from tradition in Christianity, from society, or from the world, not from the Lord. One day, however, after receiving mercy, we will love the Lord Jesus and give ourselves to Him; in this way, we will hold to truth in love, and as a result, we will grow. When we see that our dealings with the brothers and sisters are outside of Christ and are not pleasing to the Lord, we will pluck out our dealings and plant them into Christ. From that point forward, our dealings with the brothers and sisters will be from Christ and in truth.

We hold to truth by loving Christ and having fellowship with Him continually. When we live in Christ continually, our every action will come out of Him, and we will grow to the extent that we grow up into Him in all things; this is genuine growth. We have genuine growth, not by listening to many doctrines or by understanding many teachings but by having more love for Christ and by having more of the element of love for the truth. When we hold to truth in this way, we will discard anything that is not the truth.

We need to realize that truth refers to the union of God and man; we must reject anything that is not related to this union. In regard to our clothing, we should not put on anything that is not out of our union with God; we should not have any dealings with people that are not out of our union with God. We need to hold to the truth of the union of God and man in every matter so that we will grow up into Christ the Head in all things.

Ephesians 4:14 and 15 are in contrast to each other. In verse 14 the believers, as little children, have been deceived, have fallen because of craftiness, and have been carried about by winds of teaching. Consequently, they are in a system of error. In verse 15 the believers hold to truth in love and grow up into Him in all things, who is the Head, Christ. In the first situation, the believers are carried about by the winds of teaching and have fallen into the enemy's craftiness. In the second situation, they are holding to truth in love. In the first, they have entered into a satanic system of error, but in the second, they are growing up into Christ the Head.

THE GROWTH OF THE BODY

After we have experienced Ephesians 4:15, every brother and sister will come out of their culture and flesh and grow up into Christ. Then out from the Head all the Body will function and cause the growth of the Body; Christ in the Body will increase. This kind of increase causes the Body to build itself up in love. Such growth and building causes the entire Body to be Christ, to be full of the Son of God, and to be the measure of the stature of the fullness of Christ. The entire Body will be the Word becoming flesh and the flesh becoming the Word; the entire Body will be full of truth. In order for the Body to build itself up in love, there must be the functioning of *every joint of the rich supply.*

Colossians 2:19 says, "All the Body, being richly supplied and knit together by means of the joints and sinews." This shows that joints are for the supply of the Body and that sinews are for knitting together the members of the Body. Hence, when Colossians speaks of joints and sinews, it speaks of the supply and of being knit together. Ephesians also refers to the supply. In the church some of the brothers and sisters are like joints and sinews in the Body, who can supply others and be knit together with others. Because they are the joints and sinews, the Body can be properly coordinated and knit together.

The brothers and sisters who are the supplying joints in the church should not minister winds of teaching. If they minister winds of teaching, the Body will be dismembered. They need to receive the riches of the Head and the rich supply of life from the Head in order to supply all the members. Only in this way can the members coordinate with one another and arrive at the oneness of the Body. In the Body, not every brother and sister is a joint; however, some brothers and sisters are joints of supply. The building of the Body is not only through every joint of the rich supply but also through the operation in the measure of each one part. Each one part of the Body has its operation, life, function, and activity, and all the parts need to be coordinated with one another and joined to the Body. Such a Body, on the one hand, is out from the Head, and on the other hand, it is coordinated and joined together through the joints of supply and the operation in each one part. This Body builds itself up and gradually grows until it is inwardly full of the Son of God and the Christ of God. This is the goal we should attain in our service.

Colossians 2:19 shows that the growth of the church is due to the growth of God. When God grows in the church, the Body will also grow. The content of the church is Christ, and the result of the growth is that Christ increases in the church. This should be the goal of our service in the church.

As we are discussing the administration of the church, we should not focus merely on the technical aspect, like conducting an administration course. The church is not a governmental organization; the church needs Christ inwardly. If we want to administrate in the church, there is only one way, and that is to live out Christ and to minister Christ; only this is genuine service in the church. I hope that we will have more prayer to eliminate the winds of teaching so that we may hold to truth in love and grow up into Christ the Head in all things. Then out from the Head and through the supply of the joints and the operation in each one part in the Body, the Body will grow and attain to the building up of the Body.

Chapter Six

THE BUILDING AND THE ADMINISTRATION OF THE CHURCH

(4)

THE GROWTH OF THE BODY OF CHRIST

Ephesians 4:11-13 shows that the Head, Christ, gave various gifts to the church for the perfecting of the saints unto the work of the ministry, unto the building up of the Body of Christ. Verse 13 shows that the goal, the purpose, of the service and work of the building up of the Body of Christ is that we would all arrive at the oneness of the faith and of the full knowledge of the Son of God so that we may be full grown and have the measure of the stature of the fullness of Christ in the church.

The word *at* is used three times in verse 13; this does not point to three different goals but to one goal in three stages. When we lead the saints to know the Son of God, we cause them to grow in life and to have the measure of the stature of the fullness of Christ; these three things are one. The Greek word for *arrive at* also means "enter in" or "enter into." When we lead the saints, our purpose is for them to enter into the full knowledge of the Son of God and into the growth in life; eventually, the highest and ultimate goal is for them to have the measure of the stature of the fullness of Christ. To know the Son of God is the beginning, but having the measure of the stature of the fullness of Christ is the ultimate goal. Furthermore, *arrive at* in Ephesians 4 not only has a sense of "entering into" but also of "passing through," similar to passing through a box by entering one end and coming out the other end, and then entering into a second and a third box.

Verse 13 speaks of the goal of the work of the church, and verse 14 speaks of Satan's work in opposing God's goal in verse 13. The tool that Satan uses for his opposing work in the church is the wind of teaching, which causes man to follow him into a system of error. Verse 15 counteracts verse 14. Because of the opposing work of Satan, there is the need for us to hold to truth in love, to hold to the growth of Christ in the church, and to hold to God manifested in the flesh. This is to hold to truth.

The result of holding to truth is that we grow up into the Head, Christ, in all things. Formerly, nothing we did was in Christ, but now we can grow up into Him in all things because we can hold to truth in love. The meaning of *growth* in Greek denotes not merely growth but of growing up into the Head, Christ. Formerly, our entire living and all of our actions were not in Christ and were unrelated to Christ. But because we hold to truth in love, we can reach the point where our entire living and everything we do grows up into Christ.

Verse 16 says, "Out from whom all the Body, being joined together and being knit together through every joint of the rich supply and through the operation in the measure of each one part, causes the growth of the Body unto the building up of itself in love." *Out from whom* means that when we grow up into the Head, Christ, we receive a supply from Him. Those who are joints of supply are not the source but rather stations of supply; the source is Christ, the Head. The joints of supply can be compared to gas stations, but the gas comes from the refinery, which is the Head. The members who are joints receive the supply from the Head, and then they become stations of supply, each supplying the needs of the Body. Furthermore, we need to see that every member is useful; every member must manifest his function in the life of Christ.

In order for the members to manifest their function, there is the need of the supply from the joints of supply; when the functions of the members are manifested, the Body will be joined together and knit together. With the Head as the source and through the supply of the joints and the function of every member, the Body will grow by being joined and knit together. This is the increase of Christ in the Body, and as a result the Body builds itself up in love. This is also the condition of our body—out from the head, through many joints of supply and the function of every member, the body is joined and knit together and the body grows in full.

HOLDING TO TRUTH IN LOVE

Ephesians 4:15-16 uses the phrase *in love* two times. On the one hand, truth needs to be held in love, and on the other hand, the Body builds itself up in love. God is joined to man because He loves man, and man also is joined to God because God loves man. This is a great truth in the Bible. In the entire Bible, the union of God and man is altogether because of love. Without the enlightening of the Holy Spirit, it would be hard for us to understand the meaning of *in love.*

For instance, the Lord clearly said, "He who loves Me...I will love him and will manifest Myself to him..., and We will come to him and make an abode with him" (John 14:21, 23). Paul also said, "For the love of Christ constrains us...that those who live may no longer live to themselves but to Him who died for them and has been raised" (2 Cor. 5:14-15). For Paul to say that he could not live by himself means that he lived by Christ. He could not live by himself because he was constrained by Christ's love. He loved Christ and held to truth in love. He said, "It is no longer I who live, but it is Christ who lives in me..., who loved me and gave Himself up for me" (Gal. 2:20). The sacrificing love of Christ touched Paul and caused him to have a response of no longer living to himself but of having Christ live in him. Not living to ourselves but letting Christ live in us is to hold to truth in love.

Moreover, Ephesians 3 also speaks of love, "Being rooted and grounded in love...and to know the knowledge-surpassing love of Christ, that you may be filled unto all the fullness of God" (vv. 17, 19). Hence, from the Bible we can see that the love between God and man causes man to live in God and allows God to live in man. Holding to the fact of man living in God and God living in man is holding to truth. This holding to truth is in the love between God and man.

In the Old Testament, Song of Songs speaks of how a

pursuer of the Lord fellowships with the Lord, how she loses herself in the Lord, and how she allows the Lord to saturate her entire being so that she can be exactly the same as the Lord. In the end, she and the Lord, the Lord and she, are inseparable in love. The union of love (cf. 8:6-7) is their union in God's life. We are united with the Lord in love, and we also hold to truth in love.

In the book of Ephesians Paul charged the Ephesians to hold to truth in love; in the book of Revelation the Lord also brings up the matter of love. He wants the church in Ephesus to recover their first love (2:4). When a church leaves her first love, there is a danger of losing the testimony of the lampstand (v. 5) and the life of the tree of life (v. 7). *Lampstand* refers to God in man as light; *life* refers to God in man as life. If we lose our love toward the Lord, we will not be able to hold to the truth of the union of God and man. Without love, truth itself will be lost. Hence, in the entire Bible the motive for the union between God and man is love.

One who does not love the Lord or desire the Lord cannot live in the Lord; one who does not have a desire for the Lord cannot let Him have the ground in him and be everything to him continually. Only one who desires the Lord and longs after Him can allow Him to live in him. This kind of person does not want anything that does not take the Lord as the center and content; he simply loves and wants the Lord Himself. This is to hold to truth in love. Thus, if we would live in such a love and simply want the Lord Himself, we must hold to the truth of God manifested in the flesh and of the union of God and man. The more we love the Lord in such a way, the more the element of Christ will increase in us. The more there is this kind of people, the more the measure of the stature of Christ will be in the church and the more the Body will build itself up in love (Eph. 4:16).

CHRIST, THE SON OF GOD, BEING THE CENTER

We need to understand that the wind of teaching is not the "wind of pagan religions" as rendered in the Chinese Bible. This phrase in Greek refers to teaching, because the word *teachers* in Ephesians 4:11 has the same root as *teaching* in verse 14. Seeing this point is a great help to us. In the past we might have thought that the phrase *wind of teaching* refers to the winds of other religions, that is, to the deceptions of other religions. Based on the Greek, however, Paul was not speaking concerning this at all. He was referring to teaching that does not take Christ as the center in the church. We should not consider that the winds of teaching are the winds of pagan religions.

In our preaching we should never depart from Christ as the center so that our preaching of the Word and our preaching for edification do not become winds of teaching. If we want to stand against Satan's strategy, we must be according to Christ and be joined to Christ in our preaching. Whenever we are detached from Christ in our preaching, we will be void of life, and our preaching will become a wind of teaching that will blow and toss people about. If we have truly seen that Christ is the center, no matter what we preach, we will speak from Christ and return to Christ. This is like a wheel which has a center, a hub. The central point of our preaching is Christ, and this One crucified (1 Cor. 2:2). Like the wheel, it has a hub. There are also spokes that come out from the hub and the rim. There are many truths on the rim, but we cannot speak the truth from the standpoint of the rim; rather, we must speak from the center to the rim, and then return from the rim back to the center. In this way, the word we preach will not lose its center.

If we want to speak concerning baptism, we must speak from Christ as the center. This is how Paul spoke. He said, "Are you ignorant that all of us who have been baptized into Christ Jesus have been baptized into His death?" (Rom. 6:3). In contrast, many people today debate over the practice of baptism, and these debates take people away from Christ. This is the same with the matter of head covering. When Paul spoke of head covering, he began from Christ. He said, "Christ is the head of every man, and the man is the head of the woman, and God is the head of Christ" (1 Cor. 11:3). He spoke regarding head covering by starting from Christ and returning to Christ. There is no need for us to speak to the sisters concerning head covering. As long as we bring them into Christ, they will spontaneously cover their heads. If there are sisters who are against head covering, we do not need to debate with them; we must simply bring them into Christ as the center. At a certain point, they will say to the Lord spontaneously, "O Lord, I take You as the Lord of all; You are the Head over all things." At this time, they will certainly sense that they need to cover their heads. This is to speak concerning head covering starting from Christ, through Christ, and returning to Christ.

Concerning the matter of standing against the devil, we cannot skip over Ephesians chapters 1 through 5 and go directly to chapter 6. In order to stand against the devil, we must reign with Christ in ascension because we cannot stand against the devil outside of Christ. Outside of Christ, we cannot stand against the devil; rather, the devil stands against us. If this is the case, we fall into the winds of teaching, into the error of Satan's scheme and system. In Ephesians 6 the warrior standing against the devil has died with Christ, has been resurrected with Christ, and is seated in the heavenlies with Christ.

All teaching must come out of Christ, pass through Christ, and return to Christ. Even if we speak messages concerning things on the rim, we still need to begin from the center, pass through the center, and come back to the center. If a person has not seen the center, he will always speak from the rim, and his speaking will become a wind of teaching that distracts people from Christ. All of our problems lie in not seeing Christ as the center. When we see that Christ is the center, everything is very simple. Since 1934, God has gradually opened my eyes to see this. From 1944 until today, I have rarely spoken a message that is apart from Christ. No matter what I speak, I speak of Christ. If Christ is not spoken of, the message has no substance. No matter what we speak, we must come back to the center—Christ and His cross.

When we speak concerning how to administrate the church, our goal must be for the saints to know the Son of God and to discern the winds of teaching (Eph. 4:13-14). The administration of the church is the dispensing of Christ into the brothers and sisters. Some people are concerned that their preaching may become winds of teaching because of their inadequate knowledge of the Son of God, and for this reason we must firmly grasp this principle: We should speak to the level of our knowledge of the Son of God; we should never speak more than this. The Son of God is the center, and we should speak from the knowledge we have of Him. Even though sisters do not stand on the podium to release messages, in their constant contact and conversation with people, they also should not exhort other sisters, saying, "You should not wear anything red or flowery." If they speak in this way, it will become a wind of teaching. Instead, we should first let people see that the Lord is in us as life. Even though this point is simple, it is a high principle. We need to tell the people whom we contact about this, and in our testifying and conversation, we should let them see that the Lord is in us as our life. If we know only this and speak only this, it will cause those whom we contact to be blessed. Speaking anything else will become a wind of teaching. Our service in the church is to serve Christ to others; our administration in the church is to administer Christ to others. We can minister only what we have. We should minister what we have, and we should not minister more than what we have. This is a simple principle.

DISCERNING WINDS OF TEACHING

Some people may be very gifted in preaching the word, but strictly speaking, the gift is not related to preaching the word itself; instead, it is a kind of talent. After one has the central subject, there is a need for some gift. But I am afraid that if we have a gift without the center, we may become a factory that manufactures winds of teaching and an expert who creates winds of teaching. Some people are very eloquent, and their preaching always touches people. However, among those who listen to their preaching, very few rise up to pursue Christ; they are satisfied with going to heaven after salvation. It is often difficult to find even one among them who lives in Christ. May the Lord have mercy on those who speak, because they are truly experts in creating winds of teaching.

On the contrary, some are not very eloquent in their preaching, but when people listen to their preaching, they desire the Lord and want to let the Lord live in them. This kind of preaching is a preaching that holds to truth. When we fellowship with them, even though their speaking may not be so clear, it causes us to live in the Lord and pursue His life. This is what we need to treasure. Although some may be slow of tongue and clumsy in utterance, we must still bow our head and thank the Lord for preparing such brothers in the church to give us the truth, the reality.

Of course, it would be better if one has both the truth and the gift. Paul's utterance in Ephesians 4:11-16 is very good; he was truly eloquent. However, his eloquence is not a wind of teaching that carries people away. At the end of his speaking, he exhorts us to hold to truth in love so that in all things we may grow up into Christ, the Head, "out from whom all the Body, being joined together and being knit together through every joint of the rich supply and through the operation in the measure of each one part, causes the growth of the Body unto the building up of itself in love." Paul was truly eloquent; Peter could not utter such great and high truths. Paul was not only able to speak these truths, but he also lived in them so that they became his ministry.

This is what Paul is speaking of in 2 Corinthians when he said, "We have this treasure in earthen vessels that the excellency of the power may be of God and not out of us" (4:7). He said that Christ is in us and that we will be transformed into the same image from glory to glory when we behold and reflect as a mirror the glory of the Lord with an unveiled face (3:18). Even if we are enlightened, we are sometimes unwilling to die inwardly. Then the Lord will come to do a killing work in us so that even though our outer man is decaying, our inner man will be renewed day by day (4:16). Hence, we see a ministry in 2 Corinthians in which Paul not only saw some light, but he became what he saw.

Through this fellowship, I believe we should be able to discern the winds of teaching. A brother may be unrefined and without much eloquence, but he is filled with the Holy Spirit and ministers Christ to people with his speaking. This is what we want. Another brother, however, may be very eloquent, and his speaking may be very fluent, but it does not enable us to touch Christ; this is the wind of teaching. When we listen to men's preaching, even if we do not clearly receive anything, we should at least be able to discern whether it is a wind of teaching or the truth. Simply put, the truth among us should match the truth in the New Testament, which is God manifested in the flesh and the union of God and man. If a message does not have the Son of God as the content, we should immediately conclude that it is a wind of teaching. This principle will enable us to discern winds of teaching so that we will be deceived no longer.

We are not here to learn to criticize others but to learn to serve God. Whether we are learning to be elders or deacons, our service must take the Son of God as the content and center and minister Him to others. Otherwise, we will speak winds of teaching. Hence, we must first see what it means to administrate in the church. If we administrate in the church without such a seeing, we will be amateurs doing the job of professionals; we will not truly know what we are doing. We should give others our knowledge of the Son of God. If we sense that we are short of the knowledge of the Son of God, we should pray that the Lord will enable us to touch Him, to know Him as the Son of God, to minister what we have touched to the brothers and sisters, and to dispense the Son of God whom we know. In this way, even though we may not say much, what we say will be the truth, not winds of teaching.

Since we came to Taiwan in 1949, many people can testify that the messages we release have the Son of God as their content. Although we lead people to study the Bible, studying the Bible is not our main burden; our main burden is to minister Christ, the Son of God, to others. We should always have a shameful feeling before the Lord if we have not sufficiently ministered the Son of God to the brothers and sisters. Our inward burden is that the brothers would firmly grasp this principle: serving the Lord is serving others with the knowledge of the Son of God. I would rather gain ten people who know this principle than a thousand who do not.

THE GIFTS NEEDING TO DO THE WORK
OF PERFECTING THE SAINTS

When a gift serves in a particular local church, he must realize that the service in that church is the responsibility of the brothers and sisters there; it is not his business. He should not replace them in the service of God; rather, he should teach them to serve God. If he sees that a certain brother has the potential to be an elder, then in his service, he should speak concerning the eldership in several meetings; moreover, he should bring this brother into the service. In this way, responsibility will spontaneously fall on this brother. Some brothers and sisters care about the business affairs of the church and also are diligent; thus, they are suitable to be deacons. Therefore, the brother should speak something concerning being deacons, and he should also bring these brothers and sisters into the service. After he has worked in that place for a period of time, he should be able to unload his burdens onto some of the brothers and sisters. When his burdens are fully unloaded and the brothers and sisters are able and willing to pick up the burdens, he can leave. His work is to teach and to perfect the saints, not to replace them.

However, pastors in Christianity are not like this. When they are invited to a certain place, they serve God in place of the believers. This shows a great difference. If no one in your house knows how to cook, you can hire a cook to cook for you. One day, after complaining regarding the low pay, the cook may quit. As a consequence, you will have no choice but to hire another one. In different circumstances, someone who does not know how to cook can ask a famous chef to teach him how to cook, step by step, beginning with buying groceries, until he has learned all the skills. This is the way of the gifts spoken of in Ephesians 4:11. The gifts do not serve in place of others; rather, they bring others along to perfect them until they know how to serve, and then the gifts leave for another place to perfect other people. The principle of the work of the gifts is absolutely different from that of pastors and preachers in Christianity today.

All the brothers and sisters who serve God, especially the co-workers, must hold firmly to this principle: Wherever they serve, they should teach and perfect the saints instead of replacing them. I lived in Chefoo for a long time, and it seemed as if many church affairs were upon me. But when I became ill, I did not need to hand over any matters, because these matters were already in the hands of the saints. When I left, there was no need for me to call certain ones to hand matters over to them. This is because I did not replace the brothers and sisters in the service to God; in fact, they were serving regularly. I have always kept the principle of not replacing the brothers and sisters in the service; instead, I perfect them to serve. It should not be that the longer we stay in a certain place, the heavier our burden becomes; rather, the longer we stay in a certain place, the heavier the burden of the brothers and sisters should become. A gift should firmly grasp this principle.

We should not be under the influence of degraded Christianity. A gift should not be hired by any local church to replace the saints in serving God. None of the co-workers should be hired or employed by any locality to replace the saints in serving God. The proper way is for the gifts to be equipped by God and sent by God to different places to teach and perfect the saints to serve God. Everyone who serves the Lord should see this blessed light and should be so clear concerning not replacing but perfecting the saints instead. Not only should the co-workers see this, but the elders in the local churches should also learn to not replace others. The elders need to handle some matters personally, but they still need to perfect others until they also can handle these affairs; otherwise, the church in that locality will not be strong. We first must see. Then we can lead the saints to know the Son of God, to be a full-grown man, and to have the measure of the stature of the fullness of Christ.

THE BUILDING OF THE CHURCH
ULTIMATELY BEING ACCOMPLISHED

Today winds of teaching still abound, causing the children of God to be carried about. In eternity, however, God's ultimate goal, the New Jerusalem, will be reached. When the New Jerusalem appears, there will not be a broken brick or stone, nor will there be any wood, grass, and stubble. Instead, there will only be gold, pearls, and precious stones; everything will be according to God's nature, God's image, and God's glory. In actuality, from God's perspective, the New Jerusalem is here today.

Once a sister co-worker prayed in a prayer meeting, "O Lord, Your church is weak and poor and wretched." This prayer touched our feeling, but immediately after she prayed, a brother co-worker stood up and prayed with thanksgiving, "O Lord, the church is never poor and weak; the church is strong from eternity to eternity." This prayer, like thunder, was quite the opposite to the sister's prayer. I would like to ask, which prayer was right? Both were right. When we see the church from the human standpoint, the church is weak, poor, and wretched; the church is not acceptable. But when we see the church from God's standpoint, the church is not merely acceptable but strong. Even though the children of Israel fell into idolatry and fornication, God caused Balaam to bless them when he was about to curse them, saying, "He has not beheld iniquity in Jacob, / Nor has He seen trouble in Israel" (Num. 23:21). In God's eyes, there was no iniquity in the house of Jacob, and there was no trouble in the house of Israel. According to our feeling, the coming of the New Jerusalem is in the future; with God, however, it is now. God has already seen the New Jerusalem; she has gold within and precious stones without—she has God's life within and God's glory without.

Throughout the centuries all those who have God's view have said with praises, "The church is not weak but strong; the church is not poor but rich." In God's eyes we are gold, pearls, and precious stones. In the New Jerusalem there are only gold, pearls, and precious stones; there is no wood or stone. No matter how subtle Satan's stratagems and system of error are, God will eventually succeed. Today we need to stand on the way of success, not on the way of nullification. We need to do the work that holds to truth in love rather than Satan's nullifying work. This is our life and service.

CHAPTER SEVEN

THE MATERIALS OF GOD'S WORK

Scripture Reading: Matt. 16:15-19; 1 Pet. 2:5; Rev. 21:11, 18-21; 4:2-3; Gen. 2:8-12

SEEING WHAT GOD HAS ORDAINED FOR THE CHURCH

In order to conduct ourselves in the church, we must see what God has ordained for the church. If we want our service in the church to be according to God's ordination, we must first enter into God's thought in order to see what He has ordained for the church from eternity to eternity. In other words, in order to properly administrate the church, serve the church, and serve God, we must have God's view. Otherwise, our work will differ from what God has ordained.

Christ, the Son of God, is the center of God's ordination in the church. With this in mind, we need to focus on the materials that God uses to build the church in addition to how He builds the church. As such, our focus must not be on methods but on materials. We must see the kind of materials God uses to build His church. As we serve God, we should see not only the materials that He uses to build up the church according to His eternal intention but also see what He intends to ultimately obtain from His building work, including the nature of what He intends to obtain. Therefore, I do not need to stress methods and techniques; rather, I want to stress our need to see the intrinsic nature of God's building.

THE CHURCH BEING BUILT
UPON CHRIST AS THE ROCK

From the record of the Gospels we can see that even though the Lord was with His disciples on earth for quite some time and had many conversations with them, He rarely spoke of the church. The Lord did not bring up the matter of the church until Matthew 16; this is the first revelation and direct reference to the church in the Bible. Why did the Lord not speak of the church before Matthew 16? When the Lord Jesus asked the disciples, "Who do you say that I am?" (v. 15), Peter answered and said, "You are the Christ, the Son of the living God" (v. 16). Then Jesus answered and said to him, "Flesh and blood has not revealed this to you, but My Father who is in the heavens. And I also say to you that you are Peter, and upon this rock I will build My church" (vv. 17-18). The Lord spoke of the church only after He brought His disciples to the point of showing them a transcending view of Himself as the Christ of God, the Son of God. From this we can see that a person can truly speak of the church only when he knows the Lord Jesus as the Christ, the Son of God. In other words, when a person knows the Lord Jesus as the Christ, the Son of God, he can speak of the building and the service of the church.

The Lord said, "Upon this rock I will build My church," only after Peter realized that the Lord was the Christ of God, the Son of God. This is an important point: when God builds the church, He builds it upon Christ as the rock. We should not understand the Lord Jesus being the Christ, the rock, in a superficial way. We need to see that God will build His church only upon Christ as the rock. In saying that He would build His church upon this rock, the Lord meant that the rock is the foundation of the church. This rock is Christ Himself; in other words, Christ Himself is the intrinsic nature of this rock. The Lord acknowledged that He is the rock and the foundation of the church, but more importantly, He acknowledged that He would build the church upon this rock.

CHRIST BEING THE BUILDING MATERIAL
OF THE CHURCH

Christ will build the church upon this rock; the rock is the foundation, and He will build the church upon it. What, however, is the building material He uses? When we build a meeting hall, we use cement and rock as the foundation, and on this foundation we use materials such as steel columns, wood posts, and glass panes, doors, and windows. In a theological sense, some people think that the church is built by simply putting Christ together with His believers. This thought is without revelation. When Peter acknowledged that the Lord Jesus was the Son of God, the Christ of God, the Lord immediately said to him, "You are Peter, and upon this rock I will build My church." The Greek word for *Peter* means a "stone," and the Greek word for *rock* means a "mass of rock." When Peter recognized the Lord Jesus as "the Christ, the Son of the living God," the Lord immediately answered, "You are Peter, a stone, and upon this rock I will build My church." The rock refers to Christ, and the stone refers to Peter. Peter was originally called Simon Barjona, but after knowing the Lord as the Christ, the Son of the living God, the Lord changed his name to Peter, meaning that he was a stone. This is similar to the story in Genesis 32. After Jacob wrestled with God at the ford of the Jabbok, God changed his name from Jacob to Israel.

First Corinthians 15:47 says that we were earthy. Romans 9:21 says that we are also a lump of clay. Peter's original name was Simon. He was a lump of clay, but a change transpired in him. When he was in the region of Caesarea Philippi, the veil in heaven was lifted for him, and his eyes were opened. Like a camera, he received something of heaven into him; he received a revelation of the Lord Jesus as the Christ, the Son of God. When this heavenly revelation entered into Simon, he was changed from a lump of clay into a stone. The Lord said to him, "You are Peter, a stone." The inward nature of this stone is related to the mass of rock, Christ. This means that the church is produced by Christians being built upon Christ.

Formerly we were not Christ-men, but one day God opened our eyes, and Christ shined into us; then we became Christ-men. In Galatians 1:15-16 Paul says that it pleased God to reveal His Son in him. The word *reveal* in this verse is the same as in Matthew 16:17. When the Father revealed to Simon that the Lord Jesus was the Christ, the Son of God, Peter received a revelation of Christ within. With this revelation, he became Peter, a stone. This shows that the Lord builds the church with Himself as the material; He builds the church upon Himself.

We cannot take someone who is Chinese and say, "I will build you into the church." Neither can we take an American and say, "I will build you into the church." If we want to build a Chinese or an American into the church, the first step is to dispense Christ into them. If we cannot minister Christ into them, regardless of what we do, we cannot build them into the church. If we cannot impart Christ into others, they will have no way to be part of the church. In Christianity there can be false Christians, Christians without Christ, but in the church there is no such thing because all those who are built into the church must have Christ within them.

Christ uses Himself as the material and builds the church upon Himself by revealing Himself into man and then by building upon what He has put of Himself into man. In Himself Christ is Christ, but when Christ enters into us, He is built upon Himself in us, and He comes out of us, this is the church. In Himself Christ is Christ, but through revelation He dispenses Himself into us. Then upon the Christ who has been dispensed into us, He builds more of Himself; this is the church. This is the meaning of Matthew 16.

Before Matthew 16 Christ, the Son of God, was in the universe, but He was not recognized by Simon. Although He was right before Simon's eyes, He had not entered into Simon and thus could not be mingled with Simon. One day a revelation from heaven opened Simon's eyes and shined and revealed Christ to him. From then on, he had a revelation of Christ. With this revelation, he was changed from a lump of clay to a stone. The Lord seemingly said, "You are Peter, and since you are a stone, I am going to build My church. But I am going to build the church upon Myself as the rock. Once you, Simon, have been changed in nature by receiving Me, I will build My church by building you, as a little stone, upon Me, as a mass of rock." A little stone can become a part of this big rock because the rock has been dispensed into the stone. Therefore, the church is the Lord's building Himself upon Himself. The material which the Lord Jesus uses for the building is only Himself. Today the Lord is building us, the believers, into Himself.

We need to see the material the Lord uses to build the church. When we see this, we will know what material to use in the administration and service of the church. The Lord builds the church with Himself as the material; He builds Himself into men, causes them to be changed in nature, and then builds the church with the ones who have been changed in nature. We should also serve and administrate the church with Christ as the material. We must use wood to build a wood house, and we must use stones to build a stone house. Likewise, we must use Christ as the material to build the church. Only in this way will the church be Christ. According to 1 Corinthians 12:12, the church is Christ because the Body, the church, is built with Christ as the material.

In the church there is only "Peter," not "Simon"; there is only stone, not clay. Whereas clay is natural, stone is regenerated; it is produced by Christ's mingling Himself with the clay. If we have such a view, we will not bring anything natural into the church, nor will we help others with anything natural, because natural things cannot produce the church. We touch Christ by revelation, and only the Christ who has entered into us through revelation can be built into Christ and produce the church.

THE BUILDING MATERIALS OF THE CHURCH

In 1 Corinthians 3:9 Paul uses two illustrations to speak of the church: one is God's cultivated land, and the other is God's building, that is, the dwelling place built by God. Paul says that we are God's fellow workers, working together with God to build the church, God's dwelling on earth. In verse 10 he says, "As a wise master builder I have laid a foundation." The foundation spoken of here is the same as the rock in Matthew 16; the foundation that has been laid is the rock. The foundation that was laid by Paul is Jesus Christ.

At the same time, he also charged each man to take heed how he builds upon the foundation. This indicates that the building work is very particular; some build upon the foundation with gold, silver, and precious stones, and others build with wood, grass, and stubble (vv. 10-12). What is spoken of in Matthew 16 is connected with 1 Corinthians 3. The stone in Matthew 16 is part of the precious stones in 1 Corinthians 3. The foundation is Christ, but the only materials that can be used to build upon it are gold, silver, and precious stones, not wood, grass, and stubble.

Wood, Grass, and Stubble

We should understand the words *wood, grass,* and *stubble* figuratively because they are figures conveying certain meanings. Wood, grass, and stubble are all botanical, which implies naturalness. Wood, grass, and stubble all grow naturally, and they are easily burned with fire. Once they are burned, they are finished. When wood is burned, it is gone; when grass is burned, it is gone; when stubble is burned, it is gone. This indicates that wood, grass, and stubble are natural.

In the figures of the Old Testament, wood, grass, and stubble denote the nature of man. For example, the Ark in the tabernacle was made of acacia wood overlaid with gold (Exo. 25:10-11). Gold signifies divinity, and wood signifies humanity. But acacia wood is a high-quality wood, signifying the humanity of the Lord Jesus. First Peter 1:24, Isaiah 40:6-7, and 51:12 indicate that all flesh is like grass. All flesh is wood, grass, and stubble because they grow up from the ground, from clay, and are of the earth, the world. Hence, these three items denote nothing less than human nature, the flesh, and the world. All of these things are natural and cannot withstand burning or trial. If we build the church, serve the church, and work in the church with these things, then we are building the church with humanity, the flesh, and the world. If we use wood, grass, and stubble as our materials, they will not remain when they go through the test of fire.

Gold, Silver, and Precious Stones

In the Bible, gold, silver, and precious stones are all positive things; these three items are not natural. Both gold and silver must pass through the refining of fire, and precious stones are produced through pressure under the earth and through the refining of fire. Hence, these three things share a common trait, that is, they are not in their natural, original form. Wood, grass, and stubble are all in their original form; they are natural. However, gold, silver, and precious stones have passed through the refining of fire and pressure in the ground, so they are not in their original forms; they have been transformed. This can be compared to Simon's name being changed to Peter. It is like clay being changed into a stone, and a stone being changed into a precious stone through the refining of fire.

Moreover, in the Bible, gold signifies divinity, and silver signifies redemption. The Old Testament speaks of the expiation silver (Exo. 30:15-16). Hence, figuratively speaking, silver refers to redemption, and redemption refers to the cross. The cross is not only for our redemption but also for the termination of the old creation; the cross is not only for the taking away of sins but also for the taking away of the old creation. In Revelation 4:3 the One on the throne is like a precious stone in appearance; therefore, precious stones signify God's glory, God's appearance. When we serve and build the church, we cause people to receive God's life and God's nature; this is gold. We also can lead them to know Christ's redemption and the cross and to experience the cross in terminating their sins and the old creation; this is silver. As a result of the operation of these two aspects in them, they will be like God in appearance; this is the precious stone.

Hence, gold signifies God's nature, silver signifies the redemption of the cross, and precious stones signify the glorious image of God. How can we work in the church and build up the church with gold, silver, and precious stones? We need to dispense God's life into others so that they may have God's life and nature; this is gold. Then we need to lead them to experience the cross so that their sins and the old creation can be terminated; this is silver. After they experience these two points, they will live out God's image; this is the precious stone. If we continually serve and work in this way in the church, we will be doing God's work, and we will be building the church of God with gold, silver, and precious stones. Otherwise, we will be doing something natural, something of the flesh, and something of the world, which are wood, grass, and stubble.

We should serve and build the church with gold, silver, and precious stones. We should dispense God's life into others and lead them to experience the cross so that they may live out the glorious image of Christ. This is gold, silver, and precious stones. Apart from these three things, everything is natural, of the flesh, and of the world, which are wood, grass, and stubble.

Peter in Matthew 16 becomes a precious stone, who is shining, bright, and full of the glory in 2 Corinthians 3. Second Corinthians 3:18 says, "We all with unveiled face, beholding and reflecting like a mirror the glory of the Lord, are being transformed into the same image from glory to glory, even as from the Lord Spirit." When we experience Matthew 16 by receiving revelation, clay is changed into stone. The Holy Spirit, however, must still do a transforming work in us until we are transformed into the same image from glory to glory; then we will be precious stones.

As God's fellow workers, we are building the church of God on the unique foundation that has been laid—Christ. We must take heed how we build upon it by building with gold, silver, and precious stones. In the administration of the church, all of our methods or techniques will be wood, grass, and stubble if we do not see this. May God open our eyes to see that the building of the church is not a matter of method or technique but a matter of material. It is not a matter of how we work but a matter of what we use in our work. We can produce the glorious image of Christ in people only if we use Christ, God's life, and the cross.

The Holy Spirit inspired the writing of the Scriptures, and this inspiration is great and wonderful! The Bible does not put precious stones or silver first, but gold first. The sequence of gold, silver, and precious stones indicates that in our work and service in the church, we must first enable people to receive God's life and be regenerated. Then we need to lead them to experience and know the cross of Christ so that precious stones will be produced. In other words, this sequence involves dispensing God's life into others so that they may have the gold of God's life and nature. Then we should lead them to know the cross of Christ and show them that all the problems have been dealt with through the redemption of the cross. Sin, the old man, and the world have been terminated by the cross. The more a person has this kind of experience, the more he will have the element of precious stone in him, and the more he will have the glorious image of God.

Peter did not forget the word the Lord spoke in Matthew 16. In 1 Peter 2:5 he says, "You yourselves also, as living stones, are being built up as a spiritual house." This shows that he understood the Lord's word. In Romans 9, Paul likens man to a lump of clay, and in 1 Corinthians 3, he likens the believers to precious stones. Verses 14 and 15 say that all work involving wood, grass, and stubble will be consumed, and only the building that comes from gold, silver, and precious stones will remain. Then verse 16 continues, "Do you not know that you are the temple of God?" This does not refer to an individual but to a corporate entity, the church. Hence, these precious stones are the pieces of stone in the temple, and these stones are undoubtedly those who have received Christ and who have been transformed.

In Romans 9 Paul says that the natural man is a lump of clay, and in 1 Corinthians 3 he speaks of the believers, who once were natural, as precious stones. Did Paul forget his word in Romans 9 when he wrote 1 Corinthians 3? Paul did not forget, and neither did Peter. This is the reason Peter said that the believers are living stones, who are being built up as a spiritual house, which is the church. Can we build the church with doctrines or methods? No, we must build the church with Christ and the cross. We need to lead people to receive God's life and to live according to the cross. This will issue not only in gold and silver but also in the image of God—the glorious, precious stones.

THE NEW JERUSALEM BEING
THE COMPLETION OF GOD'S BUILDING

Now we must consider the New Jerusalem, which shows the completion of God's building work. In 1 Corinthians 3:9 Paul says, "We are God's fellow workers; you are God's cultivated land, God's building." All those who serve God throughout the ages are God's fellow workers. We work together with God for the building of His dwelling place on earth, and this dwelling place will ultimately become a city. In the church age God's building is a dwelling place, but in eternity it will become a city. This dwelling place is the dwelling place of God in spirit (Eph. 2:22). The city will be a dwelling place. The church in the New Testament age does not include the saved ones in the Old Testament, such as Abraham, Isaac, Jacob, and the twelve tribes of the children of Israel. The church age does not include those in the Old Testament; it includes only the saved ones in the New Testament.

Ephesians 2:20 says that the church is "being built upon the foundation of the apostles and prophets, Christ Jesus Himself being the cornerstone." This means that the church was not produced prior to the apostles' time. At that time, no stone had been built on the foundation. However, the work of building God's dwelling place did not begin only in the New Testament. We cannot say that there was no working in Abraham, Isaac, and Jacob. When the New Jerusalem appears, it will not be merely a dwelling place; it will be a city, and the dwelling place will be included in it. In this city the twelve apostles are the foundations and the twelve tribes of Israel are the gates. The New Jerusalem is the aggregate of all the saved ones in both the Old and New Testaments, and the church is a part of it; the church is a dwelling place. The New Jerusalem is a city, and the church is part of it; although the two are different in scope, they are the same in nature.

Revelation 21 clearly shows that the New Jerusalem is of pure gold; it is constituted with and full of God's life and nature. Her appearance and light are like a most precious stone, like a jasper stone (v. 11). The foundations of the wall of the city are adorned with every precious stone, and the first foundation is jasper (v. 19). Revelation 4:2-3 says that the One who is sitting on the throne is like a jasper stone in appearance. Hence, the appearance of the city is God. The city proper refers to its content, which is pure gold; the wall refers to its appearance, which is precious stones. This matches the definition in the Bible. The inward nature of those who are saved is absolutely God's golden nature, and the outward appearance is precious stones, the appearance of God. The content of the city is gold, and her appearance before the nations is precious stones; she has God's glorious nature within and God's glorious image without.

Furthermore, this city has pearls rather than silver. Having no silver implies that sin and the old creation are no longer present because the cross has terminated everything. The old heaven and old earth have passed away, and everything has become new, so there is no further need for the redemption of the cross. Because the redemption accomplished by the Lord is eternally effective and will not pass away, however, He is still called the Lamb in the New Jerusalem (21:22; 22:1). In brief, there is no part of the old creation in the New Jerusalem, so there is no need for the cross; hence, there is no silver. Redemption came in because of the fall, because of sin. But if there had not been the fall or even sins, God would still need to attain to His goal. God's eternal purpose is for His life to be mingled with man. Therefore, in eternity we cannot see redemption and we do not need redemption, because the old creation has passed away. However, we can still see God's goal, which is God's life.

In the New Jerusalem everything is God's glory, God's appearance. There are twelve gates in the city; each of the gates is, respectively, of one pearl (21:21). The pearls are gates, on which the names of the twelve tribes of the sons of Israel are inscribed (v. 12). What does this mean? First, a gate is an entrance. Without gates, we would have no way to enter into a city; if we want to enter into a city, we need to pass through the gates. We have a part in the city because of an entrance; this entrance has been passed on to us from the Jews in the Old Testament. John 4:22 and Romans 1:16 say that salvation is of the Jews. Hence, the twelve tribes of the sons of Israel represent an introduction to salvation. Second, this entrance leads us into the new city. Third, the pearl gates are produced from oysters in the sea. When an oyster is wounded by a grain of sand, it secretes its life-juice around the grain of sand and makes it into a pearl. This signifies regeneration; regeneration is an entrance. The oyster signifies the Lord

Jesus who was wounded in the sea of the world; as grains of sand, we fell into Him. From that day on, He has been secreting His life-juice around us to make us pearls. Formerly, we were sand and clay, but the Lord came to the world and was wounded; we fell into Him and have been nourished by His life. Now we are becoming pearls. This entire picture shows that there is nothing natural or of the old creation in the New Jerusalem. Everything begins with regeneration and eventually becomes God, having God's life, nature, and glory, becoming the new creation, being of pure gold and precious stones.

Since the entire city is of pure gold, the street of the city is surely of gold; this denotes that God's life and nature are our spiritual way. The more we have God's life and nature, the more we are inwardly clear concerning God's way. Our participation in this city begins with regeneration; we enter the gates through regeneration. We should consider this picture: the gates of the New Jerusalem are pearls, and upon entering through the gates of regeneration, we walk on a street of pure gold. The city proper is of pure gold, and the appearance of the city is precious stones. The meaning of this picture is that we enter through the gate and receive God's life by regeneration, and after entering through the gate, we walk on the street according to God's life and nature.

In Revelation 22 there is only one street in the New Jerusalem, and in the middle of this street there is a river of water of life, proceeding out of the throne of God and of the Lamb (v. 1). The throne is the center; the twelve gates are on four sides; the street is not straight but a spiral that goes upward. This means that if we enter through this gate, we will step onto this street; if we enter through another gate, we will step onto the same street. In the end, the street spirals up to the throne. In the middle of this street there is the flowing of the river of water of life, signifying that if we depart from the divine life, we will lose our way. On both sides of the river of water of life is the tree of life, and this tree of life is a vine that spreads and grows on both sides of the river of water of life and produces fruits continually (v. 2). In the middle of the street are the water of life and the tree of life, indicating that life is the only way. In order for God to reach the goal in His work, man must enter through the gate to obtain God's life by regeneration; then this life will continue to spiral and spread in him, and in the end, God's glorious, heavenly image will be produced and expressed through precious stones.

This is God's eternal intention. Today we need to lead people to enter the gate through regeneration. After they enter the gate, we need to show them that God's life and nature are the way they must take, and that they must eat and drink the life of God so that their entire being is filled with this life. We still need the cross, however, because the New Jerusalem has not yet come, and we are still in the church age. The cross terminates sins, the world, and everything of the earth and causes us to become pure gold. The issue of this will be pure gold within and precious stones without. This picture—the street of pure gold, the wall of precious stones, and the gates of pearl—is unveiled to us so that we may see the materials that we need for building and serving the church.

When we go to the record in Genesis before man's fall, we can see that the garden of Eden was a miniature of the New Jerusalem. In the middle of the garden was the tree of life, and a river went forth and divided into four branches. In the river flowed gold, bdellium, and onyx, a precious stone. This is a beautiful picture. In this garden was a man who was made of dust, a man of clay, and by his side were gold, bdellium, and precious stones. Genesis 2 is a picture full of meaning. God's intention is that through eating the fruit of the tree of life and drinking from the river of the water of life, Adam would be transformed to become gold, pearl, and precious stone. Sadly, the evil one, Satan, came and seduced man to eat of the fruit of the tree of the knowledge of good and evil. This distanced man from God's life. However, through the cross of Christ, God will eventually attain His goal of producing the city of gold, pearl, and precious stones in Revelation.

May God open our eyes so that we may see the work that God has intended from the very beginning and the materials He is using to reach His intention. In the process of God's work, we have received mercy to become His fellow workers. With much humility, we must work together with Him.

CHAPTER EIGHT

TEN CRUCIAL POINTS
IN THE ADMINISTRATION OF THE CHURCH

Scripture Reading: Eph. 2:13-16; Col. 3:10-11; 1 Cor. 12:12-13

CREATING THE TWO IN HIMSELF INTO ONE NEW MAN

If we want to clearly know what the church is and what God desires to do in the church, we need to understand Ephesians 2:13-16, Colossians 3:10-11, and 1 Corinthians 12:12-13. Many people have a wrong understanding of Ephesians 2; they think that it concerns the Gentiles' relationship with God. In actuality, it concerns the Gentiles and the Jews becoming one new man in Christ. Verse 13 says, "You who were once far off." This indicates that in addition to the Gentiles being far off from God, they were also far off from the Jews. The Gentiles and the Jews were in two absolutely different realms in the old creation, in the flesh. According to the old creation, the Jews were in one realm, and the Gentiles were in another; people in these two realms could never become near. They were so far off that they could not come near or have contact with one another.

In Ephesians 2 the apostle shows that these two, who could not come near and who were far off from one another, have become one new man in Christ. Thus, verse 13 says, "But now in Christ Jesus you who were once far off have become near in the blood of Christ." *You who were far off* refers to the Gentiles. The Gentiles were once far off from the Jews, but now through the redemption of Christ with the shedding of His blood, they have come near to the Jews. Verse 14 says, "For He Himself is our peace, He who has made both one and has broken down the middle wall of partition, the enmity."

Both does not refer to God and man, or to God and the Gentiles, but to the Gentiles and the Jews. Christ accomplished redemption on the cross so that both—the Gentiles and the Jews—could become one. He also broke down the middle wall of partition. What is "the middle wall of partition"? Verse 15 says, "Abolishing in His flesh the law of the commandments in ordinances, that He might create the two in Himself into one new man, so making peace." The middle wall of partition is the law of the commandments in ordinances. The law does not allow the Jews to have any dealings with the Gentiles, and because of this, there was a middle wall, there was enmity. But Christ crucified the law and abolished the enmity on the cross so that He might create the two in Himself into one new man. Christ has created the two in Himself into one new man.

In the New Testament the *new man* does not refer to an individual; there is no individual new man. The new man is a corporate new man. In other words, in the New Testament there is only one new man, not many new men, just as there is only one old man, not many old men (cf. Gen. 1:26; 1 Cor. 15:47). There are millions of people on earth, but there are not millions of old men; there is only one old man. In the same way, there is also only one new man. Hence, Ephesians 2:15 clearly says that Christ created "the two in Himself into one new man." *The two* refers to the Gentiles and the Jews. Formerly, they were separated by the law, but now the middle wall of partition has been broken down through the crucifixion of Christ. Thus, the two were created in Christ into one new man.

Verse 16 says, "And might reconcile both in one Body to God through the cross, having slain the enmity by it." This clearly shows that through the cross Christ broke down the middle wall of partition between the Jews and the Gentiles in the old creation and created the two in Himself into one new man; as a result, the two are one Body. Formerly there were Jews and Gentiles, but now the two have been created in Christ into one new man.

In Colossians 3:10 Paul uses the phrase *put on the new man*. This is not a charge that we put off the old man and put on the new man; rather, it refers to an accomplished fact. In Christ, we have put off the old man and put on the new man. We must read Colossians 3:10 with Ephesians 2:15, which says that Christ has created the Gentiles and the Jews in Himself into one new man; Colossians says that in Christ the old man has been put off, and the new man has been put on.

To put on the new man does not mean that you put on a new man, I put on a new man, and millions of believers put on millions of new men. There is only one new man, just as there is only one old man. The old man is Adam, who is in millions of people in the world. Adam, who is in millions of his descendants, is the old man. Hence, there are not millions of Adams or millions of old men; there is only one Adam, one old man. Christ, the One who is in millions of Christians, is the new man. There is only one new man. The old man is Adam; the new man is Christ. Before we were saved, we were in Adam, the old man; when we were saved, we came out of Adam, put off the old man, and put on Christ, the new man.

THE NEW MAN BEING RENEWED
ACCORDING TO THE IMAGE OF HIM WHO CREATED HIM

Although we have put on Christ and Christ is in us, the new man has not yet been manifested through us. According to Colossians 3:10, the new man "is being renewed unto full knowledge." When we are saved, Christ enters into us and we put Him on (Gal. 3:27). However, we do not have sufficient knowledge of Christ. Thus, from the day of our salvation, we are being renewed unto full knowledge. The more we believe, the more knowledge we receive; the more we believe, the more thorough our knowledge becomes; and the more we believe, the fuller our knowledge will be. This gradual renewing is according to the image of the Lord; this means that Christ has put us in Him and created us into one new man. From the day we are saved, we have put on the new man, and this new man is the same as the Lord. However, because of our inadequate knowledge of this new man, our living still does not bear the full image of the Lord.

From the day of our salvation, the new man is being renewed unto full knowledge, and this renewing is according to the image of Him who created him. We have put on the new man once for all, but our knowledge of the new man is being renewed gradually, and this gradual process of renewing is according to the image of the Lord. As we know the Lord more, the new man will be renewed more and more, and the image of the Lord will be manifested more.

Colossians 3:11 says, "Where there cannot be Greek and Jew, circumcision and uncircumcision, barbarian, Scythian, slave, free man, but Christ is all and in all." *Where* refers to the new man. In the new man there cannot be Greek and Jew, circumcision and uncircumcision, barbarian, Scythian, slave, and free man. All such distinctions are in the old man; they have all vanished in the new man. The church is not something of the old creation; the church is a new creation, and this new creation is the new man whom Christ created in Himself.

CHRIST BEING ALL AND IN ALL IN THE NEW MAN

Colossians 3:11 indicates that Greek and Jew, circumcision and uncircumcision, barbarian, Scythian, slave, and free man are on the cross. Everyone is on the cross. You are on the cross, and I am on the cross. There is no natural person in the new man. *There cannot be* is a strong word indicating that everything has been terminated. There cannot be anything in the new man except Christ, who is "all and in all." There cannot be Southerners and Northerners, educated and uneducated, in the church; there is only Christ. There cannot be you or me, and there cannot be slave or free, but Christ is all.

In the church there is only Christ; in the church Christ is all and in all. If we truly see this light, there will be such a change in our service and work! Before we were saved, we were in the old man, and we put on the old man. There were many differences among us because of all the differences that exist in the old creation. Our old man was fallen, and everything was divided as it was at the tower of Babel. One day, however, the cross came, and all the distinctions and differences were terminated on the cross. The cross nullified all the differences. After Christ terminated the old man, He created the one new man in Himself. He passed through the cross, and now nothing of the old creation exists in the new man. In the new man, there is only Christ, and He is all.

Concerning the Body of Christ, 1 Corinthians 12:12 says, "For even as the body is one and has many members, yet all the members of the body, being many, are one body, so also is the Christ." The clause *so also is the Christ* indicates that the church is Christ. Verse 13 continues, "For also in one Spirit we were all baptized into one Body, whether Jews or Greeks, whether slaves or free, and were all given to drink one Spirit." This corresponds to Colossians 3:11. Whether we are Jews or Greeks, whether we are slaves or free, we have all been baptized in one Spirit into one Body, and this Body is Christ. We have all been baptized in the Holy Spirit into one Body, that is, into one new man, into Christ.

Formerly, we were outside of the cross and in the old man, in Adam. In Adam, in our old man, there are many differences. There are Gentiles and Jews, Southerners and Northerners, educated and uneducated, slaves and free. Nevertheless, the cross has dealt with all these differences. On the cross all things in the universe have been terminated. The cross can abolish enmity and every kind of difference because the cross abolished all of the old creation and everything in it. By the cross and by our passing through the cross, Christ has reconciled His redeemed ones and created them in Himself into one new man.

In this new man there is only Christ; He is all and in all. Although there are many members in this new man, there is only one Body. In 1 Corinthians 12 those who are Jews, Gentiles, slaves, or free have all been baptized in the Holy Spirit into one Body, into the one new man. This new man, this Body, is Christ Himself; in this new man there are no differences; there is only Christ. Christ is all and in all.

TEN CRUCIAL POINTS
IN THE ADMINISTRATION OF THE CHURCH

From the various portions of the Word above, we can see what the church is. All of the serving ones in the church must see what the church is, what the nature of the church is, what God intends to build, and with what God builds the church.

Only when we are clear concerning all these points can we administrate and serve in the church.

First, in order to administrate in the church, we must have Christ revealed in us. Second, we must clearly see that Christ is our life. Third, we should realize that we must live in Christ. Fourth, we must see that what we are and what we have in ourselves has been terminated on the cross. Fifth, we must not serve or work according to what we are and what we have in ourselves. Sixth, we should not dispense anything other than Christ in our service and work in the church. Seventh, we should not expect those with whom we serve to change in any way; instead, we should desire only that they gain Christ, be filled with Christ, and be fully gained by Christ. Eighth, we must clearly see that there should be only one result in our service, work, and administration of the church. Christ must be produced in the church so that everyone has Christ, so that Christ increases in every member, and so that all will arrive at the measure of the stature of the fullness of Christ. Ninth, in order to administrate the church, we must pray for the above eight points; we must be men of prayer. Tenth, we must be like the apostle Paul who had a living faith, believing that God can accomplish these points. The first eight points constitute proper service in the administration of the church; the last two points state that we must pray and have faith, praying for the above eight points every day, believing that God is able to do superabundantly above all that we ask or think. The power of God is not outside of us but inside of us. Through the operation of the power within us, God can fulfill all these things. This is the administration of the church. If we do not see this, our service in the church will be null and void.

THE PATTERN OF PAUL

Paul is a typical example of serving; we can see all of these ten points in Paul. In his fourteen Epistles, he clearly speaks of these ten points.

First, in Galatians 1:15-16 he says that he served God because it pleased God "to reveal His Son in me that I might announce Him as the gospel among the Gentiles." He served

God in such a way because God revealed His Son in him so that he might announce Christ among the Gentiles. He announced the Son of God. He did not announce Christianity or any particular doctrines, but only Christ. Paul announced the living Christ whom God had revealed in him, not knowledge or doctrine.

In the church many brothers and sisters serve the Lord merely out of zeal or diligence, but not out of a revelation of Christ. Some people may be stirred up by their zeal but will not receive Christ through these serving ones if they do not have such a revelation. Although a serving one may believe in the Lord, he must have a clear and specific revelation concerning Christ. Paul not only announced Christ, but in Ephesians 3:8 God charged him "to announce to the Gentiles the unsearchable riches of Christ." In Galatians he says that God revealed Christ in him; in Ephesians he says that God made known to him the mystery of Christ (3:3-4). Hence, for the administration of the church, we must have a revelation of Christ.

In our preaching of the gospel, we must have a revelation of Christ. Without such a revelation, our gospel preaching will persuade people merely to join a religion and believe in some teachings. There is a hymn that says, "Rescue the perishing, / Care for the dying, / Snatch them in pity from sin and the grave; / Weep o'er the erring one, / Lift up the fallen, / Tell them of Jesus the mighty to save" (*Hymns,* #921). We cannot say that this hymn is wrong, but we need to remember that our gospel preaching is not merely to rescue sinners; rather, it is to dispense the Christ whom we have seen to others. If we do not have a revelation, a vision, of Christ, our preaching will persuade others only to join a religion and believe in some teachings. Without revelation, we cannot cause others to see Christ; without vision, we cannot dispense Christ into others. When we preach the gospel, we must have a revelation; we must be like Paul, who received revelation from God and then announced Christ among the Gentiles.

Second, in Colossians 3:4 Paul speaks of "Christ our life," indicating that he lived in God together with Christ. Third, to those who tried to work out the law by themselves, he says,

"I...have died to law that I might live to God...and the life which I now live in the flesh I live in faith, the faith of the Son of God, who loved me and gave Himself up for me" (Gal. 2:19-20). He realized that he needed to live in Christ. Fourth, Paul says, "I am crucified with Christ; and it is no longer I who live, but it is Christ who lives in me" (v. 20). This means that he realized that all that he had was terminated on the cross. Fifth, in Galatians 6:14 he says, "The world has been crucified to me and I to the world." This means that he knew that he was terminated, and that he lived in Christ. With respect to the cross, Paul was finished; he no longer lived according to his former self. Not only did Paul feel this way, but even those in the world saw him in this way. Sixth, in Galatians 4:19 he says, "I travail again in birth until Christ is formed in you." Paul's unique goal was to dispense Christ into others so that Christ could increase in them.

Seventh, in 1 Corinthians 2:2 Paul says, "I did not...know anything among you except Jesus Christ, and this One crucified." At that time there were many problems in the church in Corinth; some of the saints were fleshy, some were fleshly, and some had sinned. Paul did not expect those who were cold to become more fervent or those who were wrong to improve; rather, he had only one hope, the hope that Christ would increase in them. Among the believers in Corinth, some were fervent toward the Jewish religion, some sought signs, some sought philosophical knowledge, and some even sought spiritual gifts, but Paul preached Christ crucified. He did not care about gifts and signs; he hoped only for the increase of Christ in them.

Eighth, in 2 Corinthians 4:12, Paul says, "Death operates in us, but life in you." Paul saw that the result of his work could only be Christ and life. If he saw that the result of others' work was not Christ, he would write to admonish and adjust them (1 Cor. 4:14). The unique purpose of his fourteen Epistles was to bring man into Christ and to cause the measure of the stature of the fullness of Christ to grow in the church (Eph. 4:13). This was his only expectation. Ninth, Paul prayed for all these matters (Rom. 1:9; Eph. 1:16; Col. 1:9; 1 Thes. 1:2).

Tenth, he believed that God was able to do above all that he asked or thought (Eph. 3:20).

Paul's Epistles take these ten points as the center. In fact, these ten points can be summed up in one point—Christ. He saw Christ. He announced Christ. His work was Christ. He prayed Christ. His faith was Christ. And the result of his work, all the more, was Christ. From beginning to end, Christ was central. Christ passed through Paul and reached all those whom he served; that is, Christ was produced in them.

These ten points show how to administrate the church, but these ten points cannot be merely written on paper and become "Ten Commandments." We should not be people of the Old Testament; we should be people of the New Testament, allowing the Holy Spirit to inscribe these ten points onto the tablets of our heart so that we may live in them. This is the administration of the church, the service in the church; this is the purpose of our visiting people, preaching the gospel, and edifying others. All the elders, deacons, and those who serve in the church should follow this pattern.

QUESTIONS AND ANSWERS

Question: Can you give us some instructions on the principle of administrating the church in the aspects of life and practice?

Answer: In the aspect of life or practice, we must firmly grasp the principle of the Body. For example, if the feet cannot "take in" a message, then the mouth must fellowship with the feet after it has taken in the message. When a message is released in the church, strictly speaking, the number who hear it is not as important as the number who take it in. We do not need to pay attention to the number of people who listen to a message but to the people who receive it. In order for something to be received by the Body, it is sufficient for a representative member of the Body to receive it. As long as a representative member of the Body receives it, the entire Body receives it.

Question: When life increases, does the weightiness of the church also increase?

Answer: When life increases, the weightiness of the church

also increases; the weightiness of the church is the life of Christ.

Question: When the number of saved ones increases, does the measure of the stature of the church also increase?

Answer: No; for example, consider a glass of sweetened water. In order to increase the element of sugar, we must add more sugar into the water. Nothing is gained by adding more water instead of more sugar. In the same way, the increase of the measure of the stature of the church does not depend on the increase of the number of believers; rather, it depends on the increase of Christ. When Christ increases, the measure of the stature of the church increases. Many times, however, when we have only a little amount of sugar, we try to add more water, and in the end, the taste of the sugar is gone. Without the increase of Christ, no matter how much we preach the gospel, the flavor of Christ in the church will eventually be lost. An increase in the number of believers does not produce an increase in the measure of the stature of the church.

Often there is an increase in the number of saved ones in the church, but there is no increase of Christ; consequently, there is no expression of fullness in the church. A certain local church may preach the gospel, for example. Before preaching, there was some flavor of Christ, but after adding "two buckets of water" by beating drums and striking gongs, the flavor can be "diluted." With more drum-beating and gong-striking, "two more buckets of water" can be added, but in the end, there may be no flavor of Christ. If there is no addition of "sugar" and the church continues to preach the gospel, three or five thousand people may be brought in, but we will be able to give them only "plain water." The increase of Christ does not depend upon the number of saved ones but upon us, the serving ones. The measure of Christ in the saints is according to the measure of Christ that has been ministered from us to them. There is no heavenly "sugar refinery" that pours down sugar from heaven. Instead, Christ must dwell in us richly in order to flow out richly. All of the flowing out of Christ's life is through His Body. Therefore, we must administrate the church properly; otherwise, the more we preach the gospel, the more the flavor of Christ will decrease in the church. If there is no addition of "sugar" but only a continual addition of "water," the flavor of Christ will be lost. This does not mean that we should not preach the gospel; rather, we must positively receive Christ and be filled with Christ to allow Christ as the "sugar" to increase in us continually.

Question: How can we outwardly distinguish godliness from mystery?

Answer: Godliness means that we, God's creatures, have God's nature within and express God's image without. Having God's life and nature within and God's expression without is godliness. Mystery refers to the fact that the Creator is mingled with His creatures. This is truly a wonderful fact. However, it is a mystery because it is incomprehensible to unbelievers. Seemingly, godliness is outward, and mystery is inward; actually, godliness is not only outward but also inward. If godliness was merely outward, it would be a godliness only in appearance, not in reality.

God enters into us; this is a mystery. We have God within and God's expression without; this is godliness. For instance, electricity is in an electric lamp, and the electric lamp shines because of the electricity; this is godliness. In 1927 in Tsingtao there was an elderly sister from the countryside who, upon seeing the shining of an electric lamp, was so astonished that she asked the host for a few lamps to bring home. Electricity was a mystery to her. But the fact that electricity was in the lamp and expressed through the lamp can be compared to godliness. We may use another example. During the great persecution of the Roman Empire, the persecuted ones were truly godly because God was manifested through them. Unbelievers, however, did not understand and thought that they were too mysterious. When they saw people like Perpetua and Felicitas, they felt that they were too mysterious. Perpetua and Felicitas disregarded their fathers' persuasion, their children's crying, and their husbands' imploring, and were not frightened by any threatenings; rather, their faces were radiant. When the unbelievers saw them, they were like the country woman who marveled at the shining of the electric lamps.

Question: What is the difference between administrating a large church and administrating a small church?

Answer: Strictly speaking, there is not much difference. In both cases, before God we must know Christ, live in Christ, be filled with Christ, and allow Christ to occupy us. As we serve in the church, we need to always minister Christ to others. Regardless of whether we serve one person or a hundred people, we need to minister Christ to them; there is no difference. Whether one person receives our help or one hundred people receive our help, it is the same; there must be the increase of Christ. This is like the glass of sweetened water with a certain amount of sugar in it. If we pour half of the water into another glass, the amount of sugar will still be the same; even if we pour the water into ten glasses, the amount of sugar will still be the same. Hence, those who know the Lord do not care for the number of people with whom they work; working among many people is the same as working among a few people. Although Paul was imprisoned, he was not at all ashamed; rather, Christ was magnified in him as always and even more. Everything depends on how much Christ we have.

The measure of Christ that we have is the measure of Christ that we can give people. Whether it is one person, ten people, or one hundred people, it does not matter. If we know Christ, we will dispense Christ. Our work and service in the church should not focus on the number of people but on whether Christ is dispensed into them and whether Christ increases in them. There is no difference between one person receiving our help and ten people receiving our help. But there is a difference between people receiving our help and people not receiving our help. One person listening to our preaching is no different than ten people listening to our preaching. What matters is that the Body receives it. This is like a vaccination. A vaccine may be injected into a capillary, but it flows through the entire body. If we want to inject a ten milliliter dose of vaccine, we do not have to inject a one milliliter dose ten times; one ten milliliter dose is enough.

Question: According to what you said, is there a need only for spiritual giants in the church? How do we hold to truth in love?

Answer: There is no such thing as so-called spiritual giants in the church. Do you think that Paul was a spiritual giant? If Paul was a spiritual giant, it would be awful because he would have been a monster in the Body of Christ. Paul was a member who functioned very much in the Body of Christ. We may use this illustration. Our mouth takes in all of our food, but we cannot say that our mouth is a "spiritual giant." It is strange that even though our mouth takes in all of our food, it does not grow bigger; rather, our thighs grow quite much.

We must bear in mind that the member who receives the most also supplies the most. Our stomach receives the most, but it also supplies the most. If Paul withheld all the riches of Christ he had received, he would have become a great monster. Paul was a great receiving vessel, but he was also a great supplying vessel. Even today, he is still supplying us. Therefore, the one who receives is the one who also supplies.

We must hold to truth in love. Many people love the Lord, but they do not hold to truth. On the other hand, everyone who holds to truth must love the Lord. To hold to truth is to live in Christ, not outside of Christ. Many people, although they love the Lord, live outside of Christ. Hence, we should not consider loving the Lord and holding to truth in love as the same thing. A person may love the Lord, but he may love not according to Christ but according to himself. Did Martha love the Lord? She loved the Lord very much. But sadly, instead of holding to truth, she acted apart from the Lord. Even though she loved the Lord, she did not hold to truth. Mary, however, was one who held to truth in love. She not only loved the Lord, but she held to truth. We need to learn to love the Lord and to hold to truth in love, that is, to love according to Christ.

Chapter Nine

THE PRAYER AND FAITH
THAT A SERVING ONE SHOULD HAVE

Regarding our service to God in the church, the point of emphasis is on the kind of material we use in our service and the result of our service. We who serve in the church must see that the New Jerusalem is what God intends to work out throughout the ages. But what does God work out through the New Jerusalem? The Bible shows that God works out His own life, nature, and image through the New Jerusalem.

Therefore, whether we administrate or serve in the church, we must do it with God's life and nature; in this way our service will produce a result that is the mingling of God with man. In other words, we must build the church with Christ, building Christ into man so that our inward life and nature may be exactly the same as Christ's life and nature.

EPHESIANS 3:16-21

Ephesians 3:16-21 says, "That He would grant you, according to the riches of His glory, to be strengthened with power through His Spirit into the inner man, that Christ may make His home in your hearts through faith, that you, being rooted and grounded in love, may be full of strength to apprehend with all the saints what the breadth and length and height and depth are and to know the knowledge-surpassing love of Christ, that you may be filled unto all the fullness of God. But to Him who is able to do superabundantly above all that we ask or think, according to the power which operates in us, to Him be the glory in the church and in Christ Jesus unto all the generations forever and ever. Amen." This word helps us know how to serve God in the church and shows Paul's spirit, attitude, prayer, and faith. We should have this spirit, attitude, prayer, and faith when we serve God in the church. If we have truly seen the church and the materials that build the church, we will have this kind of spirit and attitude, and we will also have this kind of prayer and faith.

PAUL'S SPIRIT AND ATTITUDE

Why do we say that Ephesians 3:16-21 shows Paul's spirit and attitude? For example, when a brother buys a piece of land to build a meeting hall, his spirit and attitude are manifested in the whole matter related to the building of the meeting hall. If two young saints are planning to be married soon, their spirit and attitude will be filled with marriage between now and that day. Their spirit is a spirit of marriage; their attitude is an attitude of marriage. Whoever contacts them will sense the spirit that emanates from them. What they see, what they speak, and what their heart is filled with are altogether related to the matter of marriage. This is their spirit and attitude. They have a certain matter within them so that what they see, what they speak, and what their heart cares about are related to this matter. Because their entire being is filled with this matter, it becomes their spirit and attitude.

This portion of Ephesians shows that Paul saw the mystery of Christ (vv. 3-4). Thus, his spirit and attitude—what he saw, what he was filled with, what he said, and what he cared about in his heart—were related to the vision of God being manifested in the flesh and being mingled with man in order to build the church with Christ so that the church would be filled with Christ. This matter filled Paul's entire being; hence, what he saw, what he spoke, and what he cared about in his heart were related to this matter. The most precious point in this portion of the Scriptures is not Paul's prayer and faith but his spirit and attitude. After attending several meetings and seeing the church and the building material of the church, we should become so captivated and enthralled that we are eager to return to our locality. We should return so that we can work Christ into others and build Christ as the material into others so that they may become a spiritual temple for the expression of the fullness of the One who fills all in all. This should be our spirit and attitude.

The prayer in Ephesians 3 shows that Paul was fully captured by Christ. This matter, this vision, this revelation, this seeing, became his spirit and attitude. Consequently, in Ephesians 3 he had such a prayer. Based on the context of Ephesians, this prayer is not necessary. Paul prayed in chapter 1 because he was concerned that the saints in Ephesus might not understand his words; therefore, he asked God to grant them a spirit of wisdom and revelation. This is understandable. However, when he came to chapter 3, he offered another prayer. He not only prayed, but he also said, "I bow my knees unto the Father" (v. 14). Paul knelt down to pray because he was so burdened; something heavy within forced him to bow his knees unto the Father. His vision, his revelation, and his seeing became his spirit, his attitude, and his inner mood. This can be compared to a couple who will be married soon; they are preoccupied and cannot wait to be married. This is also like the people who watch ball games because they are obsessed with sports. Because Paul was obsessed with Christ, in Ephesians 3 he could not help but kneel down.

If we have seen this vision, we will be obsessed with it, and we will bow our knees unto the Father. Hence, every elder, deacon, co-worker, and everyone who serves the Lord must see a vision, a revelation, to the point that he is absolutely obsessed with it and has the same spirit, attitude, and mood of Paul. Because Paul had such a spirit, attitude, and mood, he spontaneously had this kind of prayer; he also believed that God is able to do superabundantly. All those who serve God in the church must have this kind of spirit and attitude and this kind of prayer. All of our prayers must take this kind of prayer as the center, and we should have the faith for such prayer.

PAUL'S PRAYER

In Paul's prayer, he asked that God would grant the Ephesian believers to be strengthened. His prayer was not an ordinary prayer; he described four aspects of this strengthening.

First, he prayed that it would be "according to the riches of His glory" (v. 16). What is glory? Glory is the expression of the mystery, the content within God. In the Bible, *glory* refers to God being expressed. God expressed is glory. The children of Israel built the tabernacle at Mount Sinai. When the tabernacle was erected, the glory of Jehovah filled the tabernacle, and the children of Israel saw glory (Exo. 40:34). Solomon built the temple, and when the building was completed, the glory of Jehovah filled the temple. When the children of Israel saw glory, they saw God (2 Chron. 7:3). Ezekiel 1 and 10 show that God moved in the cherubim and walked through the cherubim. When Ezekiel described what he saw, he did not speak of seeing God; instead, he spoke of seeing the glory of God (1:28; 10:4). Therefore, glory is God expressed; God expressed is glory.

Since glory is God expressed, "the riches of His glory" must refer to the expression of the riches of God's life and nature, the riches of His excellent attributes, the riches of the Godhead. All that is in the Godhead is rich, and the expression of the Godhead is full. Colossians 2:9 speaks of all the fullness of the Godhead, which refers to the expression of God's riches. The Godhead refers to what is within God, and God's glory refers to God's expression without. The expression of the Godhead is glory. For example, electricity is the intrinsic matter within an electric lamp. The expression of the intrinsic nature of electricity in the light of the electric lamp is the "glory" of electricity. When we turn on the switch, the electricity in the lamp is expressed. Therefore, the outward expression of the Godhead is glory. Colossians shows that the inward content in the Godhead is the riches, and the glory that is expressed is the fullness.

In Ephesians 3 Paul did not pray for the expression of the Godhead; rather, he prayed that God would grant the Ephesian believers to be strengthened into their inner man. The phrase *according to the riches of His glory* means that God wants to be expressed. However, because He is restricted in the believers, He must strengthen them into their inner man. God does not want to remain only in Himself; He wants to be expressed, and glory is God expressed. The Lord Jesus is

God, the expression of God, the effulgence of God's glory (Heb. 1:3). When we speak of the glory of God, we are also speaking of the God of glory. Hence, *the riches* in Ephesians 3:16 are the riches of the Godhead, and the glory as the expression of the riches of the Godhead is the fullness.

Paul asked God to grant the believers to be strengthened into their inner man "according to the riches of His glory." This means that he prayed that the riches of God's glory would enter into the believers so that they would be strengthened to an extent that others could sense God's expression. The glory of the expressed God can enter into the believers and become the strengthening power within them. In turn, they are strengthened to express God's glory. In other words, if our strength does not express God's glory, it is not the strength that is spoken of here. Some brothers are very strong; however, their strength does not express God's glory but Adam's. In the same way, some sisters are very strong, but their strength shows the flesh and their being full of will and opinions. This kind of strength is not according to the riches of God but according to the riches of their flesh.

We need to pray, "Lord, cause us not to be strong according to the flesh." Many brothers and sisters are strong in a way that shows people the riches of the flesh; on the other hand, some brothers and sisters are strong in a way that truly shows people the riches of God's glory. Hence, Paul said, "That He would grant you, according to the riches of His glory, to be strengthened...into the inner man." This strengthening is for the believers to express God's glory, that is, for God to express Himself in the believers. This prayer is exceedingly great.

The second aspect of the strengthening of the Ephesian believers is "through His Spirit." Without the Spirit, God cannot be expressed through man. The third aspect is that the Ephesian believers would be strengthened "with power" into the inner man. This means that God's power enters into man and becomes a motivating power to strengthen man. The fourth aspect is that they would be strengthened "into the inner man." This strengthening is not a strengthening of the physical body but of "the inner man." The purpose of this strengthening is that we may express God's glory, which is God Himself.

Verse 17 says, "That Christ may make His home in your hearts through faith." This result is brought about by the inner man being strengthened. Paul did not speak of Christ earlier; he only spoke of glory and the Spirit, but the issue is Christ making His home in our hearts. Throughout the entire New Testament, in speaking of Christ living in us, there is not another verse like Ephesians 3:17: "Christ may make His home in your hearts." In Galatians, for example, 4:19 says, "Until Christ is formed in you." This refers to Christ's making His home in our hearts. *Hearts* in Ephesians 3:17 is an important word, meaning that Christ can be sensed in us. He not only dwells in us, but He dwells in our heart, which has feeling and emotion. Our heart is where our feeling and emotion lie. The heart is the organ of our feeling and emotion, and it is where Christ dwells in us. The phrase *may make His home in your hearts through faith* means that when we first pursue God's glory for our strengthening, we may not sense that Christ dwells in us; therefore, we need to allow Christ to make His home in our hearts "through faith."

NOT AN OUTWARD IMPROVEMENT
BUT THE INWARD INCREASE OF CHRIST

Paul never neglected the need to work Christ into man. He was worried that even though the Ephesian believers had received Christ, they did not have a deep sense of Christ dwelling in their hearts, as far as their feelings and emotions were concerned. Hence, Paul prayed that God would grant them, according to the riches of His glory, to be strengthened with power through His Spirit into the inner man so that Christ could make His home in their hearts through faith.

It seemed that Paul was "obsessed" with the matter of Christ in us, and this became his spirit and attitude. Paul knew that Christ was not in the hearts of the Ephesian believers, even though He was in them. If someone asks us if we have Christ in us, we will answer yes. But do we truly love Him with our heart? Consider the matter of marriage. If we could see inside a couple who are about to be married, we would find that their emotions and feelings are altogether filled with marriage. Paul's prayer is not for anything other than the glory of God to work in the believers so that they, by believing into Christ and confessing Christ, will sense Christ, love Christ, and be filled with Christ, and thus Christ would make His home in their hearts.

Paul's central concern was related to Christ's being in the believers. In our work and service of administrating the church, we should have this kind of spirit, expecting that the believers will have Christ in them and that Christ will enter into them. For example, a brother may always murmur and lose his temper in the fellowship meeting. What kind of spirit and attitude should we have toward this brother? If we desire that this brother control his temper, this desire will be our spirit and attitude toward him.

In the church where we serve, there may be a brother who likes to speak and who has a bad temper, and the brothers and sisters may hardly be able to tolerate him. As a responsible brother, you may hope that he will control his temper, but if he has not changed after a few years, you may hope that he will not come to the meetings anymore lest he affect others. If he keeps coming, you may even begin to dislike him. Even though you dare not admit it, this may become your inward spirit and attitude. If a brother loses his temper in the church and you can only hope that he will control his temper, you have not seen what it is to serve in the church. Instead of hoping that he will control his temper, you should hope that he will sense Christ within. This means that he will sense Christ within and respond to Christ dwelling within him. If all the serving ones in the church are like Paul, being "obsessed" with this matter, they will not hope that such a brother would control his temper but rather that Christ would increase in him.

CHRIST MAKING HIS HOME IN OUR HEARTS

Being Strengthened into the Inner Man

The purpose of God granting us, according to the riches of His glory, to be strengthened into our inner man is for Christ to be expressed in the feeling of our heart, that is, for Him to appear to us inwardly. This requires prayer like Paul's. In our service in the church, we should not hope that people will improve or change; we should hope only that Christ in them will become so precious, sweet, and lovely and that they will sense Christ in their hearts so that Christ may make His home in their hearts through faith. The believers' being strengthened according to God's glory enables Christ to make His home in their hearts.

Being Rooted and Grounded in Love

Christ's making His home in our hearts has a result—we are rooted and grounded in love (v. 17). When Christ is touched by us we can sense His love inwardly. We can be rooted and grounded in God's love. To be rooted and grounded in love is to hold to truth in love (4:15). Being rooted and grounded in love refers to Christ's love, not our love, because He lives in us and causes us to be rooted and grounded in His love. Being rooted and grounded enables us to apprehend with all the saints what are the breadth, the length, the height, and the depth. When we are rooted and grounded in Christ, we will know the breadth, the length, the height, and the depth.

Some people say that when Paul came to this point in his writing, he was so motivated and touched by the Lord's love that his speaking was not complete. This is the view of some Bible expositors, but this is not the case. When he was writing this, Paul transcended even the universe. If we have seen how great Christ is, we will not quarrel with the brothers and sisters, much less with our wives and husbands. When Christ is in our feeling and is real in our heart, we will be rooted and grounded in His love. In such a condition, Paul said that we would know the breadth, the length, the height, and the depth. We will realize that just as God is immeasurable, the glory expressed through Him is immeasurable, and just as Christ is immeasurable, the love of Christ is also immeasurable.

What are the breadth, the length, the height, and the depth? These four words added together equal immeasurableness.

Paul said that when we know Christ inwardly and when Christ is sensed in us, we will be rooted and grounded in His love, and we will know the breadth, which is Christ. On that day, we will also know the length, which is Christ; the height, which is Christ; and the depth, which is Christ. The breadth, the length, the height, and the depth are Christ Himself. If we know Christ inwardly, live in Him, and are rooted and grounded in His love, we will see that the One who dwells in us is the breadth, the length, the height, and the depth. On that day we will apprehend with all the saints the breadth, the length, the height, and the depth. The breadth, the length, the height, and the depth are simply Christ.

Becoming the Fullness of God

Paul continued in 3:19, "And to know the knowledge-surpassing love of Christ," the result of which is "that you may be filled unto all the fullness of God." Paul was entirely captivated by this matter, and it became his spirit and attitude. When Christ has made His home in our hearts, we can apprehend His immeasurableness, and the result is that we are filled unto all the fullness of God. We who serve in the church should have this attitude, and our thoughts and prayers should be for this.

In administrating the church, all the responsible brothers must take this as their spirit, their attitude, and their hope. They should not hope merely that all the saints will come to the meetings, be zealous, preach the gospel, and bring people to salvation. The responsible brothers should be clear as to what they take as their goal: is it an increase in numbers or an increase in Christ? They should be like Paul, who was totally "obsessed" with this matter. We need to receive mercy not to think that it is sufficient for the brothers and sisters only to be zealous and come to the meetings. Even if all the people in Taiwan came to the meetings and were zealous, it would mean nothing if they did not know Christ inwardly.

We should hope that Christ will make His home in the believers through faith, that they will be rooted and grounded in the Lord's love, and that they will come out of their small and finite beings and see the immeasurableness of the Lord.

Our hope also is that the believers will know the Lord as the breadth, the length, the height, and the depth so that they may be filled unto all the fullness of God. Then they will reach the glorious and rich goal of God to be glorified and expressed in the church. This is the apostle's prayer, which represents his spirit and attitude.

THE PRAYER THAT A SERVING ONE OF GOD SHOULD HAVE

We should focus on this matter to the extent that we do not know what to pray other than this. We cannot pray in a habitual way, saying, "O Lord, Brother So-and-so is cold. Please make him fervent. O Lord, Sister So-and-so is backslidden; please restore her to the meetings. Sister So-and-so has a poor temper; please cause her to change." Paul did not pray this way; instead, he prayed, "God, grant the believers, according to the riches of Your glory, to be strengthened into their inner man, that they may know and experience Christ inwardly, that Christ may make His home in their hearts, that they may be rooted and grounded in His love, that they may see the immeasurable Christ living in them, and that they may be filled unto all the fullness of God." This should be the attitude, spirit, and prayer of one who serves God.

PAUL'S FAITH

Perhaps some may say, "It is not easy to pray that the brothers and sisters would be fervent and rise up to meet. How much harder will it be to pray for them to be filled unto all the fullness of God? This is too ideal, too difficult." Hence, verse 20 shows Paul's faith. He spoke of "Him who is able to do superabundantly above all that we ask or think, according to the power which operates in us." *Power* is a great word in the Bible. This power is not objective, far from us and vague; this power is subjective. When we are saved, the power in us is able to do superabundantly above all that we ask or think.

This verse is not concerned with outward material blessings. For example, if I ask God to prepare a three hundred square feet house for me, and He gives me a four hundred square feet house, this is seemingly above what I ask or think. A sister, who does not have any children, may pray, "O God, have mercy on me. I do not have any children. You are the God who answers prayer; please give me a son." When God answers her prayer and she not only has a son but twin boys, this is seemingly above what she asked or thought. If a brother needs $400 and the Lord gives him $600, this also is seemingly above what he asked or thought. But this is not the meaning of this verse.

Because Paul was concerned that the Ephesian saints might think that the prayer in verses 16 through 19 was too difficult, he immediately followed with verse 20, saying, God is "able" and "above all that we ask or think." In the end, he praised God for being glorified in the church and in Christ Jesus. *Glory* in verse 21 means that God is greatly released and expressed in the church; this is glory. God being glorified in the church means that He is fully expressed in the church. No matter what our present condition is, we should have the faith that the New Jerusalem will eventually be manifested. At that time, we will see that the glory of God illumines the city, and the lamp of the city is the Lamb; light shines forth from the lamp to illumine the entire city (Rev. 21:23).

The full meaning of the phrase *to Him be the glory in the church* is seen in the New Jerusalem. On that day, God will shine forth all of His fullness. In the New Jerusalem, nothing is opaque; even the gold is like clear glass (v. 18). Christ is the lamp of the city, and God in Christ shines forth from the New Jerusalem to all the nations. The New Jerusalem is the complete expression of God's glory; the church today should be a miniature of the New Jerusalem. This is the spirit, attitude, prayer, and faith with which we should serve the Lord. We should have such a prayer and faith. Our spirit and attitude should be that the brothers and sisters will have Christ inwardly, that Christ will make His home in their hearts, and that they will be filled unto all the fullness of God. At the same time, based on this spirit and attitude, we should pray, bow our knees, and have faith before God.

In this way, our service in the church will be great and glorious. Although this service is great and glorious, we still need to keep in mind that it depends on the God who is able, and it is God who works day after day. Galatians 4:19 says, "Until Christ is formed in you." The word *until* does not mean that God is not working but that God has been working and is working continually until the work is done—until Christ is fully formed in us. If we have such a strong seeing, it will become our spirit, attitude, prayer, and faith. If all of our spirit, attitude, prayer, and faith are for this one thing, the brothers and sisters will be filled unto all the fullness of God.

Witness Lee was born in 1905 in northern China and raised in a Christian family. At age 19 he was fully captured for Christ and immediately consecrated himself to preach the gospel for the rest of his life. Early in his service, he met Watchman Nee, a renowned preacher, teacher, and writer. Witness Lee labored together with Watchman Nee under his direction. In 1934 Watchman Nee entrusted Witness Lee with the responsibility for his publication operation, called the Shanghai Gospel Bookroom.

Prior to the Communist takeover in 1949, Witness Lee was sent by Watchman Nee and his other co-workers to Taiwan to ensure that the things delivered to them by the Lord would not be lost. Watchman Nee instructed Witness Lee to continue the former's publishing operation abroad as the Taiwan Gospel Bookroom, which has been publicly recognized as the publisher of Watchman Nee's works outside China. Witness Lee's work in Taiwan manifested the Lord's abundant blessing. From a mere 350 believers, newly fled from the mainland, the churches in Taiwan grew to 20,000 in five years.

In 1962 Witness Lee felt led of the Lord to come to the United States, settling in California. During his 35 years of service in the U.S., he ministered in weekly meetings and weekend conferences, delivering several thousand spoken messages. Much of his speaking has since been published as over 400 titles. Many of these have been translated into over fourteen languages. He gave his last public conference in February 1997 at the age of 91.

He leaves behind a prolific presentation of the truth in the Bible. His major work, *Life-study of the Bible,* comprises over 25,000 pages of commentary on every book of the Bible from the perspective of the believers' enjoyment and experience of God's divine life in Christ through the Holy Spirit. Witness Lee was the chief editor of a new translation of the New Testament into Chinese called the Recovery Version and directed the translation of the same into English. The Recovery Version also appears in a number of other languages. He provided an extensive body of footnotes, outlines, and spiritual cross references. A radio broadcast of his messages can be heard on Christian radio stations in the United States. In 1965 Witness Lee founded Living Stream Ministry, a non-profit corporation, located in Anaheim, California, which officially presents his and Watchman Nee's ministry.

Witness Lee's ministry emphasizes the experience of Christ as life and the practical oneness of the believers as the Body of Christ. Stressing the importance of attending to both these matters, he led the churches under his care to grow in Christian life and function. He was unbending in his conviction that God's goal is not narrow sectarianism but the Body of Christ. In time, believers began to meet simply as the church in their localities in response to this conviction. In recent years a number of new churches have been raised up in Russia and in many eastern European countries.